CONSTANCE SPRY

DRIED & ARTIFICIAL

FLOWER ARRANGING

Flowers for a Niche

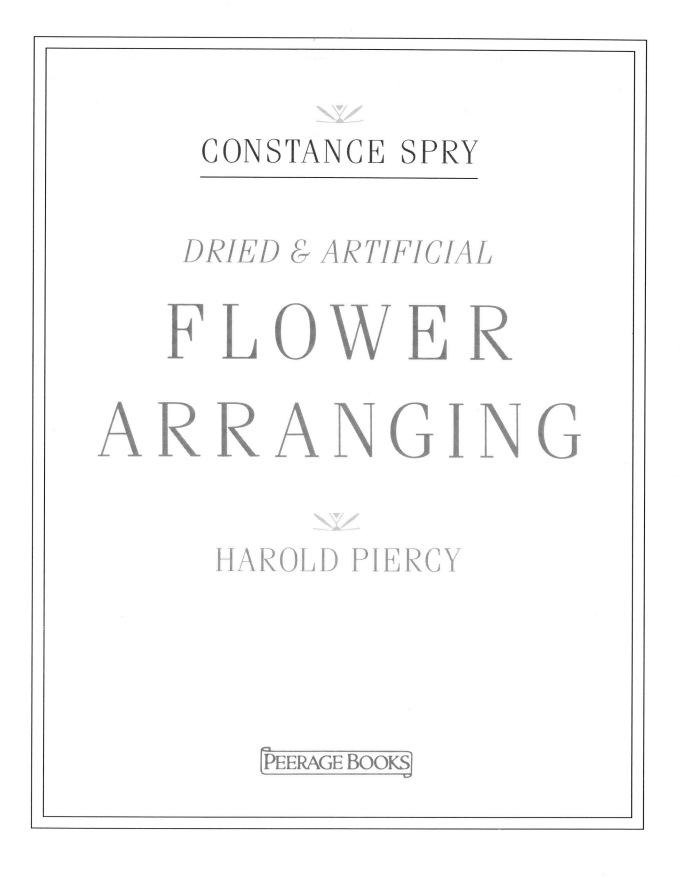

CONSTANCE SPRY

DRIED & ARTIFICIAL

FLOWER ARRANGING

HAROLD PIERCY

PEERAGE BOOKS

First published in 1987 by
OCTOPUS BOOKS LIMITED
81 Fulham Road
London SW3 6RB

© Text: The Constance Spry and Cordon Bleu Group Limited

© Photography and Illustration: Octopus Books Limited

ISBN 0 7064 2825 0

Reprinted 1988

Printed by Mandarin Offset in Hong Kong

ACKNOWLEDGMENTS

Editors	Andrew Jefford, Tony Holdsworth, Isobel Greenham
Art Editor	Pedro Prá-Lopez
Stylists	Marian Price, Maria Kelly, Vicky Wood
Picture Research	Julia Pashley
Production	Shane Lask
Illustrations:	Anne Baum/Linda Rogers Associates (pages 12, 26, 40, 62, 98) Berry Fallon Design (pages 32, 56)

The publishers wish to thank the following organizations for their kind permission to reproduce the photographs in this book: Heather Angel 19; Michael Boys Syndication 1 above right; Linda Burgess 1 below right, 1 above left; Tony Stone Worldwide 1 below left; Wildlife Matters 17.

Special photography by **Steve Lyne** (pages 21, 23)
All other photographs specially taken by **Jan Baldwin**.

The publishers would like to thank the following people and companies for their kindness in providing the materials and equipment used in the photography for this book:

Chattels (Dried Flowers and Rural Items), 53 Chalk Farm Road, London NW1 8AN
Monique Regester (Handmade Waxed Paper Flowers), 143 Talgarth Road, London W14 9DA
Joanna Sheen (Pressed Flower Pictures), Victoria Farm, Stokeinteignhead, Newton Abbot, South Devon TQ12 4QH

and

Next Interiors, 160 Regent Street, London W1
Penhaligon's, 55 Burlington Arcade, London W1
Neal Street East, Neal Street, Covent Garden, London WC2
Annabel Carter, 201 New Kings Road, London SW6
Patio, 155 Battersea Park Road, London SW8 4BV
H. Andreas Ltd., Unit 2, 44 Colville Road, London W3
Continental Imports (Mr Christmas Ltd.), Prestige House, Mowbray Drive, Blackpool FY3 7UR
Arthur Curtis (Chapmans), 327 New Covent Garden Market, London SW8 5NJ
Baker & Duguid, 287 New Covent Garden Market, London SW8 5NJ
Multiflora, 364 New Covent Garden Market, London SW8 5NJ
Florimax, 325 New Covent Garden Market, London SW8 5NJ
Holland & Evans (Flower Importers), Chesterton House, Chesterton, near Bridgnorth, Salop
Durnsford Plastering Services, 22 Weir Road Industrial Estate, off Durnsford Road, London SW19 8UG
Hayman & Hayman, Antiquarius Stands R1/H3, 135 Kings Road, London SW3
Gallery of Antique Costume and Textiles, 2 Church Street, London NW8 8ED
Symphony International B.V., Schepenveld 12–10, 3891 KZ Zeewolde, Netherlands

The publishers would like to thank the following for their kindness in providing locations for photography:

Chattels (Dried Flowers and Rural Items), 53 Chalk Farm Road, London NW1 8AN
Harold Piercy
Sue Shenkman
Don Cockburn
Andrew & Bosia Jefford

AUTHOR'S ACKNOWLEDGMENTS

As usual, this book has been very much a team effort and many people have been involved in one way or another. I would especially like to thank Rosemary Minter who helped organize the materials needed for photography, attended many of the photographic sessions and did some of the arrangements for me. I would also like to thank Julie Grosse and Sue Barrett, my back-up team at the Constance Spry and Cordon Bleu office, for their excellent typing and sorting. Many thanks, too, to Fred Wilkinson and Gayle Derrick at Winkfield; to Jenny Webb for her notes on drying flowers using a microwave oven; to Philippa Eve, who helped Rosemary and Gayle with the "fun" flowers, and to all my friends and neighbours who have helped with materials.

CONTENTS

FOREWORD

Many people would love to be surrounded by flowers in their homes or at work, but because they are busy and have no time to look after them properly, they tend to go without flowers altogether.

This is a shame, the more so as there is little reason these days not to enjoy the enormous pleasure flowers can bring. Dried and artificial flowers are the perfect answer to a hectic lifestyle: they need little attention, other than dusting and changing from season to season, yet they bring those touches of grace and colour to an otherwise familiar interior that only fresh flowers could match, or better.

The range of dried flowers that can be bought nowadays is unprecedented: supplies are available from all over the world, and there are few varieties that a keen collector could not acquire with determination and persistence. For those who like to grow and then dry their own materials, the widespread availability of simple drying and preserving media, like silica gel and glycerine, means that a huge range of fresh flowers and foliage can now be successfully saved for use in long-term arranging.

There has been something of a revolution in the world of artificial flowers, too, with the advent of polyester silk. When used by top-quality manufacturers to produce flowers and foliage closely modelled on their natural counterparts, this material can give extremely lifelike results. No one need be ashamed of using artificial flowers: I even saw an arrangement of polyester silk freesias recently at an exhibition held in conjunction with the Royal Horticultural Society!

In addition to a wealth of arrangements using dried and artificial flowers, I have also included a number of long-lasting arrangements using fresh materials. Many flowers and foliages will last at least a month, if properly arranged and maintained, and even the busiest of us could find the occasional half-hour or so that it takes to bring fresh colours and scents into the home.

I trust I've made my point and you now feel that there's no excuse for not brightening your surroundings with some of these time- and labour-saving options. My only remaining hope is that the pages that follow will serve as adequate inspiration and instruction on putting this into practice – and that you have as much fun trying out my ideas as I have had writing about them and arranging them for photography.

Harold Piercy

INTRODUCTION

Most people would agree that there is no real substitute for green plants and fresh flowers. Unfortunately, many of us are denied the pleasures they have to offer because the money and time needed to purchase, arrange and maintain them are simply not available to us.

This is when long-lasting decorations can be the answer – dried and silk flowers need little attention other than an occasional dusting and perhaps a seasonal change of materials; even moving the same arrangement from room to room provides variety. They are perfect for anybody leading a busy life.

The Uses of Artificial Materials

I'm well aware that there are many gardeners and flower-lovers who feel uncertain about bringing such items into the home. My own early training was in horticulture and I had never come across artificial flowers in any form until I joined the Constance Spry Flower School as a student. It was there that I first came across hand-made flowers used for Christmas decorations, and I found them marvellous. The quality of the work that had gone into the blooms was superb, and I realized that they more than justified their place in the home. Judge for yourself from the pictures on pages 85–86.

There are, in fact, some people who actually prefer artificial plants and flowers to their real counterparts. They may not feel very confident with growing plants and would rather go for a good imitation, knowing that the only thing they will have to worry about is keeping it clean. There's nothing wrong with this. In any case there is a right place in the house for everything, and an artificial plant, if correctly displayed, can give as much, if not more, pleasure than a real one. Many dark areas, for example, may simply not be suitable for living plants or cut flowers, and here artificial plants come into their own. The secret for a realistic effect is to imitate the growing plant as closely as possible, in particular by trying to get some movement in the stems. The reason why so many artificial flowers on the market look unreal is because they are made on very straight stems – to simplify the packing – and they are then arranged with no easing or modelling of the stems.

You'll also find many of the cheaper plastic sprays on sale far from lifelike, both in colour and shape. Avoid them and go only for the best. They may cost more initially, but will be well worth it in the long run. One final suggestion: if you're not happy with your artificial flower arrangements, you can always try using artificial blooms with real foliage as a background. You will be amazed at how many people will be completely taken in by this.

In the arrangement opposite, the autumnal colours of dried flowers can be seen at their best. A large variety of materials has been used, including celastrus berries, osmunda, moluccella, fagus (beech), crocosmia, rhododendron (azalea), echinops (cardoon flowers), rosa (yellow roses) and peonies.

Some people argue that dried flower arrangements won't stand up to scrutiny in the same way that fresh flowers will, and to some extent this is true. None of the blooms will be quite as perfect, and while single fresh flowers look very attractive on their own, a number of dried flower heads need to be used to get the same effect. The colours of dried flowers are always more muted than those of fresh flowers, though close observation will reveal that the same range of colour is still there. Many effects, if properly done, can be very soft and charming.

Timing is an important factor for success – being able to find the right material at exactly the right stage. The best way to do this is to watch plants and flowers closely, and see how they behave both in the garden and when cut and arranged in vases. You'll notice, for example, that some will dry partially before dropping. These are the best ones to work with: flowers that quickly shrivel to nothing are not often successful. Other good possibilities are flowers with stiff papery petals or bracts, or flowers that retain some of their colour when they wither.

Seasons are obviously important in this respect, though there is a great deal more flexibility to seasonal drying than one might imagine. So many people, for example, only think about drying for the winter at the end of the summer, and forget that spring is also a season well worth bearing in mind.

You will find that many of your ideas for materials will come simply from observing nature. Every time you go for a walk, keep a look-out for branches, lichen, or anything that might offer a possibility for an arrangement.

And now a word about cost. It's worth bearing in mind that, although many dried and artificial flowers seem initially expensive, they will soon pay for their initial outlay if they are carefully maintained. Dried arrangements will be a real economy during the two or three winter months when fresh flowers are at their most expensive and they will certainly keep well in centrally heated homes.

As with everything else, success with dried and artificial flowers is very much a question of trial and error. The important thing is to keep trying until you get the effect you want. I hope that this book will give you some good ideas and practical advice on the subject. But before tackling these ideas, it's important to define the terms "dried" and "artificial". The distinction may seem rather obvious, but it's surprising how easily confusion may arise.

Dried Flowers

Dried flowers are far from being artificial. They're made up from natural flowers, leaves and seedheads which have been preserved in some way. (Some are mounted on false stems, but even these are made from real materials.) Dyed varieties have recently become available, due to popular demand for certain colours; personally I would always counsel the choice of natural colours if at all possible.

One interesting innovation is shown and described on pages 53–55: botanically false flowers that have been produced using true, dried materials.

Dried flowers were very popular in Victorian times, when they played an important, though rather specialized, part in room decorations, both in the form of small posies and as intricately fashioned flower pictures set in solid wood frames.

Artificial Flowers

There was a time when the phrase "artificial flowers" would have immediately put me on my guard, but recent years have seen a great deal of progress in this area and today there are a number of extremely effective and useful materials on the market.

Artificial flowers are not a modern idea; they have, in fact, been around for years. The earliest versions were made from metal and – later – thick brown paper which was decorated with oil paint. Colours were strong and hard and the texture of the flowers was very stiff.

Constance Spry herself saw the need for good artificial flowers as far back as the 1940s, and so she started a very successful business creating and selling hand-made waxed paper flowers. These were modelled from real flowers. Two examples of these can be seen on pages 85 and 86, and on pages 88–93 there are three examples of Monique Regester's work. Monique carries on this fine tradition today.

The first of the new artificial flowers to come in to vogue after World War II were made from plastic and imported from the Far East. Many of them were machine made and mass-produced; simple in design, they were crude to the last degree. Some of the shapes were incorrect and the colours repellent; only a few of the greens, yellows and pinks could pass for anything remotely resembling real flowers and many "copies" of particular varieties were in anything but the right colour. Despite all this, however, their novelty value ensured good sales for a short time.

However, the introduction of polyester silk flowers over the last decade has made a big difference to the quality of artificial materials available. For the first time, there is movement in the stems and petal tissue, and a huge range of different flowers and foliages have become available. When movement and different shapes are incorporated into their fabric artificial flowers really come alive.

Starter Collection

Here is a list of ten varieties of dried materials that might form a starter collection, suitable for a wide variety of arrangements. In drawing this list together, I have tried to think back many years to when I first started using dried materials, with the aim of including the ones that were the most useful. Experiment with these for a while; you will always be able to find some other oddments to add interest and variety to each group. As your skill grows, you will probably want to refer to the Glossary (pages 126–141) where a more comprehensive list of materials suitable for preservation is to be found.

ACHILLEA (yarrow) This is an easy herbaceous perennial to grow – it does not mind continued picking and grows well for years. It requires an open sunny position and fairly deep soil. The flower head of the main branch of the family is flat and yellow but there are also white and lilac varieties. Foliage colourings vary from dark green to grey. They all dry well by hanging up to air-dry or by dusting with borax and laying flat in a box. The smaller heads can be treated with silica gel.

ALCHEMILLA (lady's mantle) This hardy herbaceous perennial provides wonderful green colours in its dried form, as in its fresh. It has very interesting foliage with tiny star-like petals making up a mass of small flowers. It grows well in partial shade and under moist conditions. The flowering period is May–August and if cut fully at this time you may get further flowering again in October or November. It seeds easily and soon becomes permanently established. Alchemilla is excellent for filling in space at the base of a group, providing colour and hiding the bare stems of taller specimens. Hang up to air-dry when the flowers have just opened.

DELPHINIUM (larkspur) This annual is a most useful flower because of its attractive slender flower spikes. Flowers are produced in a wide range of colours from deep pink to deep blue, cream and white. Easy to grow, in warmer areas it can be sown in autumn to provide an early crop the next year. It can be used on its own in mixed colours or with many other differently shaped flower stems. It dries very easily: hang upside down to air-dry. The individual flowers may be pressed for picture work and the main stems can be cut up into small pieces for filling in small vase work.

ERYNGIUM This is one of my favourite dried flower materials. It is a must for the garden of any dried flower arranger: it grows easily and almost dries on the plant. Choose an open sunny site with well-drained soil. Some of the varieties have wonderful colouring, such as the striking metallic blue colours covering the flowers, bracts and stems of Eryngium alpinum. I love them as a focal point in arrangements, as you will see from the number of times when I have used them in the groups photographed later in the book.

GRAIN AND GRASS HEADS I have cheated here in making a single group of plants of many different botanical families but all serve the same purpose in arrangements. They all add height and lightness to a group; each one has an interesting shape and none of them are difficult to slip into an arrangement, thanks to their stiff slender stems. I have in mind wheat, oats, barley, fox tail, quaking grass etc. All of these can easily be air-dried.

HELICHRYSUM It is the annual forms of this large genus of five hundred species that I have in mind for this list – those that bear the famous "straw" flowers from midsummer onwards. Cut when just opening – don't wait for the full centre to show. They will open more fully as they dry. As they are not easy to wire after they are dry, I would suggest that you wire them soon after picking. Leave about 1 inch (2.5 centimetres) of stem and insert the wire so that it goes right into the flower head but does not show. Once wired, stand up in bunches to air-dry. If you wish to leave the flowers on natural stems, remove most of the leaves and then bunch the flowers hanging upside-down, so that the weight of the heads keeps the stems straight.

HYDRANGEA This is a wonderful flowering shrub. The range of colours available is astonishing: it varies from a green/white through pinks, reds, purples, blues and pewter colours. Once established, hydrangeas are prolific and almost take over parts of the garden. They benefit from rich soil and like partial shade with plenty of moisture. Leave the flower head on the plant to mature before attempting to dry. This will give you a wider range of colours because these change as the flower heads become older. When cutting, take care not to remove too much of the plant because this might check the following year's flower growth. The flower heads are lovely both on their own, as well as with mixed groups of flowers. Hang up to air-dry, or dry in a little water in a warm place.

LIMONIUM (statice) There is a wealth of plant material available for drying in this genus, but it is Linonium sinuatum (a perennial, but best results are obtained when grown as an annual) that is truly invaluable to the dried flower arranger. With good quality seed and quick growing in open sunny ground one should get a good range of colour for harvesting in the autumn. It air-dries very well.

PAPAVER SEEDHEADS (poppy) or NIGELLA SEEDHEADS (love-in-a-mist) will provide interesting shapes in any group of flowers. Both poppy and love-in-a-mist can be hung up and easily air-dried: in fact if you are late harvesting and there has been a spell of dry weather they will almost dry on the plant. The poppy seedheads have a bloom to them giving blue, green and grey colouring. Nigella have green, brown and red colouring. The leaves must be removed from the poppy stems before attempting to dry, while the collar of feathery leaves on nigella may be left to add interest. Both are very long-lasting and worth having.

ZINNIA I have had such success with drying zinnia flowers in sand and silica gel that I want to encourage readers to try. The small button type, those with flowers up to $1\frac{1}{2}$ inches (3.5 centimetres) wide, are the best. Cut off with a stem 1 inch (2.5 centimetres) long and treat in really dry sand or silica gel. Wire up either before or after drying and cover the false stem with green tape.

Cleaning Flower Materials

Dried flowers are brittle and will need handling with great care when cleaning. Carefully take each stem out of the vase and blow away the dust, wiping any flat surfaces gently with a sponge or damp cloth. Sort the stems out into types and stand them in containers until each and every stem has been cleaned – plastic cartons with a little gravel in the base are ideal. Then rewire or replace the holding unit in the vase you intend using and start the arrangement again. You can take this opportunity to add new material for a change of arrangement.

Ideally, you should be using dried materials from autumn to early spring, by which time garden plants will have started growing into leaf and you can put away your dried material for another year. Stored carefully, your stock of dried flowers should last for a number of years.

Artificial flowers readily attract grime and dust – and immediately lose all their loveliness and colour. The amount of cleaning they need depends a great deal on where you keep them. If kept in relatively dust-free conditions your arrangements should last for three to four months without too much attention, save an occasional dusting.

Plastic flowers that have become very dirty can be soaked in warm soapy water – a good washing-up liquid should lift the dirt. Brush the folds and ridges of the flowers with a soft brush to remove the dirt then rinse thoroughly under warm water and hang them up to dry straight away.

Flowers made entirely from polyester silk should wash well. Dip them into warm soapy water and agitate them to loosen the dirt, then rinse in clean water. Shake them well to remove any excess moisture and hang them up to dry in a warm place, with freely circulating air.

Handmade waxed paper flowers are very delicate and need handling with the greatest of care. Each petal or leaf must be wiped over with a small swab of cotton wool soaked in a little methylated spirit, then wiped over again with a dry cotton wool pad. Be sure not to crack the wax surface.

Containers for Arrangements

Choosing the right container for dried and artificial flowers requires careful thought, but at least you don't have to worry about whether it holds water.

The suitability of different containers for specific arrangements will be dealt with in detail later, but at this stage it might be useful to take a brief look at some of the containers on the market, and consider their advantages and disadvantages. There are no hard-and-fast rules here, but bear in mind that flowers and container should work together to create the right overall effect.

KEY TO ILLUSTRATION

1 Brass scale pans
2 Shallow copper pan
3 Shallow ceramic bowl
4 Brass jug
5 Shallow copper trough
6 Sussex trug basket
7 Pewter measure
8 Terracotta troughs
9 Cream ladle
10 Upright ceramic vase
11 Ceramic bowl
12 Shallow copper saucepan
13 Indian brass pot
14 Alabaster tazza
15 Metallic Georgian-style urn
16 Terracotta pot
17 Terracotta pot with metallic finish
18 Pewter tankard
19 High-handled basket
20 Brass tankard
21 Pewter chalice

A Collection of Containers for Arrangements

WICKER AND CANE BASKETS

To many people, baskets are the obvious choice for dried flower arrangements. Charming though baskets are, they do tend to have one drawback – they're often light, and tend to over-balance easily. To overcome this, simply place some shingle, sand or even a piece of lead on the base of the basket to weight it down. If you do this, though, you'll need to line the basket first: generally a small bowl or plastic tray in the base will be adequate to this task. A good rule of thumb when buying is to bear this in mind and choose a basket with a good flat, level base.

Baskets come in many shapes, sizes, and styles. You can also, surprisingly, get them in many different shades of brown. Some are even two-tone. All will lend themselves particularly well to the straw, yellow-bronze and green colourings that are so common in dried flowers. I find the Sussex trug (which, though a basket, is actually made from wood) a very useful shape that will take dried or artificial flowers happily.

WOODEN CONTAINERS

Wooden containers are another useful group that always gives pleasing results. I find rougher surfaces are more suited to dried flowers than the more refined old pieces such as tea caddies or polished work boxes, which tend to partner silk flowers successfully.

Recent newcomers to the market are the round, flat containers made from sections of branches of the cork oak – they're set up with resin bases and can look very natural, as can be seen from the bottom right-hand arrangement in the picture opposite.

PEWTER CONTAINERS

Pewter can vary a great deal in colour, but I think it is particularly suited to mauve, pink, blue and grey coloured flowers in general. There is nothing nicer than a large mixture of hydrangea heads in metallic shades set in a fairly deep pewter bowl. Other flowers that invariably look handsome in pewter containers include larkspur, echinops, limonium (statice), eryngium and eucalyptus.

SILVER CONTAINERS

I think silver looks too grand for dried flowers unless it's old in which case it seems to acquire a softening patina and then blends well with dried materials.

COPPER AND BRASS CONTAINERS

Both are excellent complements for all those yellow, orange and beige/brown colours that so often recur in seedheads and dried flowers. Again many different shapes and sizes are available, but on the whole the old pieces are much more pleasing than many of the modern, stamped-out forms. Incidentally, old brass and copper cooking utensils make lovely containers: do look out for them.

POTTERY AND CERAMIC CONTAINERS

Pottery and ceramic containers come in a very wide range of shapes and colours and a great deal of choice is available. The very dainty or ornate pieces will look better with artificial flowers, while dried varieties call for the more rugged and heavy items.

OTHER MATERIALS AS CONTAINERS

It can be surprisingly easy to make your own vases using ordinary household waste such as tins or bottles. Choose good shapes, free from dents, and cover with a good quality Japanese straw paper, pretty wallpaper or even lining paper which may then, if necessary, be painted a suitable colour.

Soapstone and alabaster are also useful possibilities: they make interesting and unusual containers and have colours that complement dried materials in particular very well.

Five Basic Arrangements

From time to time during the course of this book, you will come across terms like "facing arrangement" or "all-round arrangement". The photograph opposite gives you a clear visual idea of what five of these basic arrangement types look like; it will provide a ready point of reference should there be any doubts in your mind as to what might be meant by one of these terms. At the back can be seen, from left to right, a facing arrangement, a basket arrangement and a spherical arrangement, while at the front left is a table centre arrangement and at the front right an all-round arrangement.

Of these different types, the ones that you will find yourself using again and again are the facing and all-round arrangements. A facing arrangement, as its name suggests, is one that is to be viewed from the front only, while an all-round arrangement looks attractive from every side. There are many examples of both in the book. Facing arrangements are generally used for shelves, mantelpieces and wall niches, while all-round arrangements make attractive decorations for side tables, sofa tables and so on. Always remember that you will need more materials for an all-round arrangement than you will for a facing arrangement. A table centre arrangement is useful for a long rectangular dinner table: you'll find a detailed discussion of this type on pages 74–75. Basket arrangements work particularly well with dried flowers, as the soft warm colour of wicker makes a perfect foil to the muted colour range of dried materials; you'll find several arrangements of this type in the next chapter of the book. Spherical arrangements, too, make attractive vehicles for dried flower material, whether in the indoor tree form shown here (there are several more examples in the next chapter), or as hanging spheres (see pages 42–44.)

Five Basic Arrangements

CHAPTER ONE

DRIED FLOWER ARRANGEMENTS

Collecting Materials for Drying

Contrary to popular opinion, you don't necessarily have to have a garden in order to acquire a good selection of drying materials. There are many alternative sources you can turn to, each of which will help to give you a wider range and, therefore, a more interesting group of materials to choose from. Woodlands, downlands, moors and the edges of lakes and ditches all provide fertile habitats for different forms of plant life and should all be studied. But the most important things to remember are never to miss a chance of adding to your collection, and to be open to all possibilities, however unlikely they appear. For instance, a railway embankment is one of the most fruitful areas in which to find material – but, of course, be careful and don't go near the track. In the main, plants can grow undisturbed there and they actually thrive on well-drained and open terrain such as this. In my many years of train journeys to and from London, I've often taken the opportunity, as the train waits at signals, to study the surrounding flora. It's amazing how many different types of plants can be seen through the year.

Waste-land or building sites are another possibility. Much of this land is changing hands these days, and there are times when you'll easily be able to glean seedheads and grasses from such places without causing any trouble.

Edges of fields and roads are also useful sources. Just make sure you consult the owner beforehand, remember the "country code" and all should be well. I've never had any problems myself and have always found people most helpful whenever I've asked if I may pick anything.

Try not to make collecting a last-minute job in late autumn. If you collect your materials earlier, you will be able to carry summer flowers, as well as autumn varieties, into the winter period when they will be much appreciated.

You can, of course, collect materials all year round but do remember to try and preserve only those materials that are perfect. All materials tend to shrink and become slightly distorted as they dry and only the best quality specimens will keep their beauty after this type of treatment. For instance, don't waste expensive glycerine on foliage that is badly shaped or eaten by grubs. Always be sure, too, to prune any branches you want to preserve, removing unwanted stems or foliage first. Don't treat anything that you know you won't have any further use for.

The materials you collect during the winter months are most likely to be seedheads. These will, in fact, be perfectly dried already. Spring is somehow not a season that many people think of as being a good time to dry flowers in, yet many spring bulb flowers will preserve perfectly in desiccants. Flowers such as muscari and fritillaria will make wonderful seed pods and will need to be collected at the correct time (pick muscari in mid- to late summer and fritillaria in early summer). As your interest in dried flowers and collecting grows, your eye will become trained to look out for this type of material.

One thing is for sure: whichever season you're collecting in, you certainly won't be short of things to put in your "drying box" – just make sure that whatever you find is free from surplus water when you bring it home (avoid collecting after showers of rain), and that you get started on drying it straight after picking. Don't keep any plant materials waiting: they will start to wilt before you even begin treating them. The fresher, the better. Dry a few flowers each day and study the results so that you learn all the details for another year.

Allium Flower Heads

Once you have collected the materials you require, you have next to dry them. There are a number of methods for doing this, and you should be careful to choose the right method for the materials you have: full instructions are to be found on pages 20–24.

Once bitten by the collecting bug there'll be no stopping you. There will be no end to the possibilities for collecting and drying you will discover and the challenges you will enjoy. You'll find that no two years are ever the same at a given time because of variables such as temperature fluctuations and changes in precipitation. It's only through experimenting, of course, that any of us can learn.

One option you may like to consider when collecting your materials is using them for pressed flower arrangements. Over the years this craft has reached a very high standard and, once pressed and dried, your materials will last indefinitely, provided that they are laid out in an arrangement, then covered with either glass or a protective laminate coat. They will fade in strong sunlight, but then most things do. For some examples of just how effective really skilful work of this sort can be, see Joanna Sheen's pressed flower pictures on pages 70–71.

Growing for Drying

If you are lucky enough to have a garden, you will be assured of a constant supply of flowers and other materials to dry and preserve. You may, however, have to plan your garden with these requirements in mind. If you simply pick flowers for preserving as and when you need them, you are sure to end up with a very bare garden for much of the year. Similarly, removing dead flowers from plants immediately will encourage the plant to grow more flowers, which is fine, but it will also mean that you won't have any seedheads, since they will not form if the dead flower is removed too quickly.

The solution to both problems is to set aside a special area of the garden for growing materials that are specifically intended for cutting and harvesting to form the basis of a dried flower collection. It's a good idea to grow these plants in nursery rows. In this way

you'll have complete control over them, and tasks such as staking, disbudding and tying up can easily be attended to as and when necessary. This system will also ensure that you get perfectly shaped stems and good flowering heads.

If your garden is too small for cutting crops, you could, perhaps, run an allotment, and give one half over to fruit and vegetables, and the other to specialist flowers such as larkspur, nigella, achillea, molucella and amaranthus that you will need time and time again for use as dried material. Any surplus material left over after drying may well be accepted by your local florist, providing that it's of good quality. Quite often this type of material comes onto the market packed in such large quantities that smaller retailers are loath to buy. Your home-grown surplus may be just what they're looking for.

Growing from Seed

Many of the commercial plant materials that are dried for flower arranging are grown as annuals – from seed sown and harvested within one year.

When growing crops from seed, you're unlikely to be in a position to be able to choose your soil, but ideally, it should be fairly open and light in texture which means that it must also have enough organic matter to be able to retain some moisture. Soil that's too rich in plant food will produce excessive leaf growth at the expense of flowers which will be very late in developing. On the other hand poorly nourished soil will bring about stunted growth and earlier flowering with small unhealthy blooms.

An annual plant has one main purpose in life – namely, to reproduce itself, so the sooner it can flower and set seed the better. Like all growing things, young plants should grow and develop steadily from their very earliest days, with no setbacks. Often, with plants grown in open ground where there is little or no control over environmental conditions, the weather will turn cold or very dry after sowing or planting out, and this will check plant growth. It's not always easy to gauge this, but on the whole, a slightly later start followed by good growing conditions will be better than an over-early start followed by a long cold spell that will set back plant growth.

Prepare the ground in late autumn and during the winter. Check the soil and if it's acid, apply a little lime. As a student I was always taught that lime can be considered the key to the plant food store room – if it isn't present in the soil, essential plant nutrients will remain "locked" in so that the plant roots cannot obtain them. Lime isn't actually a food in itself, but its reaction on minerals in the soil enables them to provide plant nourishment.

If you're growing your materials in a cutting area of the garden, make sure the rows are far enough apart to be able to use any equipment you need between the rows.

Always go for very high quality seed and sow it thinly and evenly. There should be no competition for space, which occurs when seeds are sown too thickly and cannot be thinned at the correct time. In the garden, after a good rainfall, simply pull out any unwanted seedlings. Sowing too thickly is a complete waste; the unwanted plants cannot be re-used and seed today is far too expensive to throw away.

It goes without saying that your plants will need regular watering, feeding and weeding. They must also be kept free from pests and diseases so that they're in absolutely perfect condition when they're cut for drying – a particularly important consideration, since they always deteriorate slightly during preservation. Hoe regularly to keep the soil open and dust with a little plant food towards the end of the growing season. Staking and tying will be necessary for all tall plants if you want straight stems. Always try to attend to this before it becomes really necessary – once a plant has gone over it will be virtually impossible to straighten again, and bent stems are difficult to hang up and dry.

CUTTING

As soon as your flowers are fully developed, cut them carefully. Often, taking out the main stem will induce side shoots to flower, and in a good long summer a second crop of flowers may be harvested from plants started early in the season. This is one of the advantages of sowing some hardy annuals in the autumn and growing them over the winter – if they come through well and are kept in good order then they will certainly produce a heavier crop. You must, however, have good, deep and well-drained soil that will encourage growth in early spring.

SOWING IN BOXES

This is quite simple, as long as certain procedures are observed. First, you must have a high-quality compost of good texture that provides an adequate and balanced supply of food and is free from all harmful organisms. Soil from your own border, however well-tended, will not be suitable for this particular situation – there will, no doubt, be weed seeds present, and in most cases the structure of the soils will not be properly balanced.

There are many commercial composts available. I would always go for a mixture of a good loam, moist peat and sharp sand – this will retain moisture while remaining open in texture. It should also contain chalk and plant food for maximum plant growth.

The compost should be freshly made. Use it in small quantities and replace it with fresh when required – garden nurseries with a quick turnover are probably the best places to buy from.

Heracleum Flower Heads

In order to grow, seeds must be provided with moisture, warmth and air. The art of sowing seeds in boxes successfully is to provide these conditions so that all the viable seeds will start to grow as soon as possible and make good plants. Use standard seed boxes where possible. A seed box $2\frac{1}{2}$ inches (6.5 centimetres) deep – preferably made of wood and with good drainage gaps – is best, but plastic seed trays are quite useful too. If you're going to use them time and time again, make sure you buy the best. Those with a large capacity will prove the most useful.

To fill a seed box, place it on a flat bench against the heap of fresh compost, then draw two to three good handfuls of the compost into the box. Level it and lightly press it against the corners, then completely fill the seed box, scraping off any surplus compost with a straight-edged knife. Tap each end of the box sharply on the bench three times to settle the bottom level of the compost.

Firm the top of the compost with a "presser" – ideally a piece of wood half the size of the box with pegs $\frac{1}{2}$ inch (1 centimetre) from the base to stop the presser going down too far. This will give an even, level seed bed which is firm, but springy to the touch. Sow the seeds evenly on this surface, allowing equal space for each seed to give ideal growing conditions. If the seed is sown too deeply it will take longer to germinate; if not sown deeply enough, the seedlings will fall after germination or simply not grow.

For large seeds, spot sowing at regular intervals across the box will give the best results. A useful piece of equipment for this is a template with holes drilled in it. Simply place the template on the seed bed, drop a seed into each hole, then remove the template. Cover the seed with a thin layer of compost passed through a fine riddle or sieve with an $\frac{1}{8}$ inch (3 millimetre) grist mesh, giving approximately $\frac{1}{8}$ inch (3 millimetres) of cover soil over the whole box.

Do not firm the soil, but stand the box in a shallow tray – about 1 inch (2.5 centimetres) deep – of water for a few minutes to allow the soil to become moist. Then drain the soil and place the box in a greenhouse or frame covered with a sheet of glass – preferably cut to the correct size. Finally, cover with a sheet or two of newspaper.

The paper should be removed as soon as the first seedlings show. The glass should come off shortly afterwards and before any seedlings touch it. This is a very important stage in the growth of the seedlings. You must allow them plenty of light and water with great care at this time.

As soon as the seedlings are large enough to handle they should be pricked out into boxes 3 inches (8 centimetres) deep, filled with a rich compost. Handle the seedlings very gently, loosening them carefully from the seed bed, then lift them from the soil by the seed leaf, not the stem.

Mark out the new seed box carefully, allowing equal space for each seedling. Make a hole with a blunt stick the thickness of a pencil and carefully place the seedling in this, pressing slightly to firm.

If you are saving seedlings of different sizes, try to grade them into different boxes so that they grow evenly. After pricking them out, water them carefully and replace them in the greenhouse or frame, making sure they get plenty of light.

You can gradually harden them off ready to plant outside in the border or cutting bed as soon as conditions are suitable, i.e. when frost is unlikely. Once again I must stress that the plants' growth should not be impeded at any time.

Methods of Preserving Flowers

There are six main methods of preserving flowers: air-drying, water-drying, drying in a microwave oven, using powder or desiccants, preserving in glycerine or pressing. Try them all and see which suits you the best. You may find some work better one year and others the next, simply because the growth rate and moisture content of plants varies from year to year.

AIR-DRYING

This is an excellent way of preserving flowers. It is, in fact, nature's way – we've all walked through gardens in the autumn and seen seedheads and flower stems with papery-looking flowers which have dried naturally. Air-drying takes time to do but is worthwhile, as there are many flowers that will keep well when treated this way.

There are several ways of air-drying flowers; some should hang upside down, while others may be stood upright to dry, so that they will keep their shape and in many instances a great deal of their colour. Dry slowly is the rule of thumb for most things – if dried too fast they will become very crisp and brittle and therefore awkward to handle.

There are many different grasses, all so useful as background material with which one can display the bolder dried or artificial flowers. Cut these before they form seeds so that they will not disintegrate. Tie bunches of grass together with a knot that may be tightened as the stems dry out, otherwise you will find they fall to the ground from bunches hanging upside down. Alternatively, try a tight rubber band, then a string tie above it. Remember that your flowers when dried will never have the full intensity of colour of fresh flowers but they will have a charm of their own. The pink colours seem to fade, while blue, bronze, orange, and yellow retain their true colour well.

WATER-DRYING

Water-drying sounds at first like a contradiction in terms, but in fact it's one of the best drying methods for certain flower heads like those used for the arrangement shown on page 25, or the hydrangeas on page 111. It is a very simple drying method, too: all that has to be done is to arrange the flowers in 2 or so inches (5 centimetres) of water, and then gradually let the water evaporate without topping it up. By the end of this process, the flower head will have dried.

DRYING IN A MICROWAVE OVEN

Microwave ovens can be a great help in drying flowers, particularly when you have a lot of materials that you need to dry quickly. In addition to the oven, you will need some cardboard boxes or glass or pottery trays, and quite large quantities of silica gel. Place 2 inches (5 centimetres) of silica gel in the bottom of each container, then position the flowers, stem down, in this. Cover the flower heads gently with more silica gel crystals. Place a half cup of water in the oven with the box or tray, then "cook" in the oven on 100% power for 2–4 minutes. Leave the flowers in the crystals for some time after this – overnight if possible.

SILICA GEL

Desiccants like silica gel can be very expensive and must be therefore used sensibly. Silica gel is probably the most important of these: it works quickly and well and tells you what it is doing at the same time. It is a brilliant blue when really dry and as the moisture is taken out of the petals it turns pale and then, finally, pink. It can be changed back into full strength by placing in a slow, warm oven. Once deep blue again, store in an airtight container.

Silica gel is excellent, but care must be exercised when using this drying agent. I first bought it in crystal form and found this too heavy to use – it may be all right like this kept in a small container in a box of dried flowers where it will serve a useful purpose, but I would not advise its use in this form on fresh flowers. Put the crystals in a coffee grinder or similar device to produce a powder, but be careful not to inhale the fine dust given off in the process because it may prove dangerous.

Store materials preserved in silica gel in plastic boxes with lids. Small round polythene storage canisters are excellent for individual blooms. Use small labels on the top to list details of the contents and the date of drying.

Using this method can be time-consuming, not to mention the waste involved with materials that don't turn out well and have to be discarded. You need quite a large stock of silica gel, because each flower head must be completely covered with it. You lose a little on each flower and a small amount will certainly be blown away each time or lost as you transfer the

Air-Drying Flowers and Seedheads

silica gel from container to container. So there are a number of disadvantages; as I said above, though, the results are excellent.

BORAX

Borax is a fairly cheap desiccant which tends to leave a white deposit on petals. Use it as fine dust over the whole surface. Apply it carefully – it will not easily reach the base of petals because the particles of powder don't run down like sand granules. It can be mixed with sand (using one part borax to three parts sand) to give a quicker drying time.

ALUM

Alum is another powder one may use as a drying agent. Like borax, it is not very easy to get deeply into flowers with many petals and it is difficult to clean off when petals are dry. You will need a fine paintbrush and a steady hand to dust them off. Again, it is not quick-acting like silica gel.

SAND

I feel this has a great deal to recommend it. Be sure to get fine silver sand, which is clean, rather than builders' sand which you will have to wash thoroughly and dry before you use it. I think the best way to buy silver sand is in large bags. Although it is sold as dry, it must be dried further before use.

My method for doing this is to fill old enamelled washing-up bowls three-quarters full of sand and heat them in a slow oven. I then keep them in a warm place until needed so that the sand is both warm and dry. Remember, sand is very heavy so it must be used with care but when dry the fine particles do penetrate into the flower petal bases. Depending on the structure of the flower, one should lay the flowers flat or face down and then slowly fill them in with the sand – some people allow it to trickle through their hands on to the flower. I prefer to shake a small teaspoon of sand at a time on to the flower because I find I can control the flow better this way. If you like, you can use a mixture of sand and borax to speed up the drying process. I have found that dusting borax or alum over the flower through a fine sieve before covering with sand is quite useful – it mixes into the sand and both can then be heated up for use again.

Some people recommend placing the sand and flowers in a sealed box to dry but if you have a warm boilerhouse, as I do, an uncovered box will be just as good and any moisture in the sand is more likely to be drawn out. Once the flowers are paper dry you must store them carefully. Ideally, this should be in a dry place with plenty of room, where everything can be boxed and kept clean. It's good idea to place sachets of silica gel in each box to keep out any damp. I like to lay the flowers in boxes but I know that others prefer to stick them into oasis, standing upright. Whichever you choose, above all remember that the flowers are now very fragile and must be handled with the greatest of care.

PRESERVING WITH GLYCERINE

This is a fairly straightforward process which should be carried out well away from anywhere you are drying material – you don't want moisture coming off the jars of solution to affect your other drying operations adversely. Any materials that you wish to preserve in glycerine should be in perfect condition when picked. Stems that show autumn colour before they are cut from the bush will have gone too far and will only disappoint you by dropping their leaves. Autumn colouring only starts once the food/water supply is cut off to the leaf and is nature's way of causing leaves to fall – once this natural seal is formed it will be impossible to get glycerine up into the leaves. Don't thin the branches out too much, but remove any unwanted or damaged leaves or surplus branches. Good short pieces will be useful fillers, though, so treat some of these.

The solution Mrs Spry used to recommend was 50% glycerine to 50% hot water, but some of the thinner-leaved trees and shrubs will work well with a solution of one part glycerine to two parts hot water.

Prepare the base of the stems by splitting or hammering. Then stand the stems in a fairly narrow container with 4–6 inches (10–15 centimetres) of solution in it. Make sure you allow the materials plenty of room in the container.

PRESSING

Pressing is a useful method of preserving foliage for use in arrangements, and preserving flowers for use in flower pictures. Most foliage for use in arrangements will be too large to be preserved in a flower press: my method then is to place the foliage carefully between sheets of newspaper, and position these under a carpet. For information on pressing flowers in flower pictures, see pages 68–71.

Four Drying Methods

The four drying methods photographed and described below and on pages 20 and 22 will, when mastered, provide you with a wonderful store of dried and preserved materials. (For an illustration of air-drying, see page 21. You may also like to experiment with drying in a microwave oven, and with pressing flowers and foliage.) These methods are not difficult to learn, though success with desiccants and sand improves with practice. Remember that not all materials are suitable for all drying methods: it would be very difficult, for example, to dry hydrangea flowers in sand. As you read this book, you will soon develop an understanding about matching drying methods to freshly picked material.

SILICA GEL (above left)

A desiccant that gives excellent results, particularly in terms of holding the original colour of the fresh flower. Make sure that materials are dry before use, then carefully sprinkle and cover with crystals. (For very delicate materials, grind crystals to a powder first.) Gel will turn pink when moisture-charged: heat through to dry, when the crystals will revert to their original blue.

GLYCERINE (above centre)

An effective method of preserving foliage and some flowers, giving an attractive, slightly glossy finish. The flower or foliage is stood in a mixture of glycerine and water, which it takes up as it normally would water; the glycerine in the solution then preserves the plant tissue. Make sure, therefore, that the material is still young and fresh enough to be taking up water before you begin to preserve in this way. Glycerine can be expensive if used extravagantly: trim material before beginning so that you only preserve the pieces you require.

SAND (above right)

Fine silver sand is an excellent desiccant: as good as silica gel for the right materials, and considerably cheaper. It can also be dried out and re-used endlessly. Make sure that both sand and flower material are dry before beginning. Avoid using sand for delicate material: it is heavier than silica gel and may crush the flower. Drying techniques are as described for silica gel and other desiccants.

WATER DRYING (left)

Water-drying is perhaps the simplest of all drying methods. Flowers suitable for this treatment can be picked in their fresh state, arranged as fresh, and given a little water: they will then dry slowly over a period of months with no further attention required on your part.

WIRING

Many people prefer to wire their flowers before drying them (though not, of course, if the flowers are to be dried in a microwave oven). I must admit that it is much easier to do when the stems are robust and fresh and will still take a wire, in many cases internally, but I do find wires a nuisance when trying to dry in desiccants. You have to wrap them round in a roll under the flower when the flower faces upwards or have them sticking up when the flower is facing downwards – both are awkward. Once the flower is dried, however it is very difficult to get a thin wire into the head without doing some damage to the delicate petal tissue.

Both methods have advantages and disadvantages. Frankly the most successful results come from the wiring-first method, for all its inconveniences. As usual the best idea is to try both methods and use whichever one suits you best.

SOME DRYING TIPS

● A number of seedheads, such as those of alstroemeria, should not be dried too quickly because the seed pods tend to explode. It is sensible to varnish them to help hold the seed case together.

● Seed pods which are full of seed should be stood upright to dry so that the seed may be saved. When nearing the bursting stage, you could place a small bag over each head to catch the seed.

● When out collecting seedheads and materials for drying, leave well alone if in doubt as to the identification of a particular flower. Many of our wild flowers are on the decrease due to new farming and cropping methods and use of chemicals, so please take every precaution to preserve our wild flowers. (It is, of course, illegal to pick protected species.) We have been very careful with all our work for the book to observe the law in this respect.

● Remember that plants are made up of anything from 75–95% water so when drying in sand or silica gel, this material will soon become charged with water. Dry it again quickly. Always start with your drying agent 100% dry – otherwise you will get disappointing results.

● When air-drying, time will certainly be saved if unwanted leaves are stripped before the stems are hung up to dry. The leaves come off more easily when green and the stem will dry more quickly.

● One thing worth noting when drying material in sand is that if you take out the flower before it is really dry it will shrivel and be useless very quickly. Watch progress carefully and, if in doubt, shake a little sand away and then add fresh dry sand to the flowers for a few more days.

● A towel rail, connected to a hot water system, that is not always fully occupied is a good source of quick air-drying. Place metal hooks over the chrome bars and hang bunches of flowers or foliage on to these.

A Before-and-After Arrangement

I thought it would be useful to include this "before-and-after" arrangement (see photograph opposite) to demonstate a number of points that I have been discussing over the last few pages.

It shows, first of all, the sort of changes you can expect your material to undergo in its transition from fresh to dried. A lot of the shapes have altered, and the whole colour range of the materials has changed from green/yellow to red/olive/brown. It also shows the simplicity of water-drying (see pages 22–23): the fresh materials from Southern Africa shown on the left-hand side of the photograph are accompanied by a very similar group on the right, bought exactly one year earlier. They were simply arranged in a little water, and left to dry slowly. The colour and shape changes that one can see quite clearly in the photo-graph take place imperceptibly, over a number of months. (It is perhaps worth mentioning that, if the materials had been dried in a desiccant like silica gel, the colours of the fresh materials might have held better, should this be the effect you desire. Remember, too, to display out of direct sunlight to achieve rich final colours.)

You can see how well pewter works in relation to dried flower material – these pewter tankards are among my favourite containers for dried flowers. Finally, it illustrates a point that I cannot stress often enough: materials for dried flower arrangements, although initially expensive, are in fact excellent value when one takes into account the length of time the arrangement will be displayed for, giving continuous pleasure.

Materials and Equipment

BUCKETS

There are many sizes and shapes of plastic buckets available these days. Make sure you have a good selection of sizes, taking into consideration both height and base area. They should stand firm with an even base. Most of the time buckets are used for holding dry silver sand.

CAMEL-HAIR BRUSH

Ideal for lightly touching up any petals with particles of sand or borax still stuck to them. A cheaper brush will also prove useful for applying spots of glue.

GLUE GUN

Many florists these days use glue guns for directing spots of glue on to specific surfaces. Up till now I have been very much against them, considering it to be a pretty poor state of affairs if one cannot control and fix flowers in the normal way without having to resort to a glue gun. I have, however, modified my ideas somewhat, since – once control of the gun and the flow of glue is mastered – this is an excellent way of attaching dried-up stem tissue to a wire. Stemless flowers that have been pressed can be mounted easily by simply gluing their backs to a wire stem. If you

A Before-and-After Arrangement

tried to wire these in the normal way the petals would immediately shatter.

These guns are not cheap and you will need a great deal of practice before you'll acquire the confidence to use one on good quality materials. Ideally, a quick drying, clear glue should be used with a glue gun – follow manufacturer's instructions.

A successful way of glueing the flower to an artificial stem is as follows: first cut the stem, then cut a little triangular shape at the stem top. If any of the real stem is left on the dried flower, thread this through the hole in the artificial stem, then with a spot of glue hold the base of the petals on this triangular shape. Allow the glue to dry. (This will only take a few seconds – far faster than one really would wish at times, and there is no way of getting the material free once glued.) Now fashion the material in a lifelike way and get a little bit of movement into the false stem.

HAIR SPRAY (LACQUER)

Spray this lightly on fluffy heads to hold them together and stop them disintegrating. It is ideal on bulrush and clematis seedheads.

HIGH PRESSURE AIR CANISTER

Use this to blow away dusty sediment from surfaces treated with alum or borax. It must be handled with great care. If used with too great a force, it will blow the petals cleanly off the flower head. Available from shops selling photographic equipment.

PLASTIC BAGS

Plastic bags and small plastic containers with lids are useful for treating individual flowers in a desiccant. (Small sandwich boxes and kitchen storage jars are also excellent). Always label and date each item, and

depending on the moisture present in the plant tissue, but by noting and keeping records you can then arrive at some sort of chart which will help you for drying in the future. It's very important to gauge drying time accurately – if left too long the petals will shrivel and the plant will become too brittle.

SCISSORS

The ordinary, all-purpose flower scissors that you use every day will be fine for work with dried flowers as long as they are strong enough to cut through any of the wires you may need to use for false stems.

SECATEURS

These are available today in many sizes and strengths to cut through varying thicknesses of material. A medium-duty pair would suit most people's purposes and I would recommend the type with one cutting blade and an anvil action rather than the "parrot beak" type. When using secateurs, always cut with the blade uppermost. It's better to make two or three cuts rather than wrench and twist the secateurs to get through thick material. For larger branches and stems, use a small pruning saw.

KEY TO ILLUSTRATION

1 Bottle containing glycerine	9 Crepe paper binding
2 Oasis foundation shapes	10 Gutta tape
3 Secateurs	11 Flower press
4 Scissors for ribbon and fabric	12 Reel wires
5 Wire scissors	13 Pliers
6 Wires in wire tidy	14 Oasis tape
7 2 in (5 cm) gauge netting	15 Glue gun
8 Ribbons	16 Glue
	17 Silica gel crystals
	18 Hair lacquer

Useful Equipment

WIRE

Florist's wire comes in two forms: stub wire (in lengths) and reel wire. The stub wires are used for mounting flower stems and foliage, while the reel wires are generally used for binding materials together. Remember when buying wire that the higher the gauge, the thinner the wire.

SHARP PENKNIFE

This will be useful for trimming up thick bark should any cut you have made not be really clean, as well as for general trimming and finishing of loose or frayed stem ends.

TWEEZERS

A lot of fine work is necessary for fiddly jobs like making false stems and arranging small pieces of pressed flower material when making pictures. Tweezers are ideal for holding the short piece of real flower stem while manoeuvring into position.

VARNISH

Use this to preserve attractively coloured fruits and berries. It may also be useful on ordinary seedheads, and even fluffy seedheads such as clematis if applied before the seed is ripe and really fluffy. Use a small brush and best quality clear varnish.

Dried Foliage on a Teak Pedestal

It isn't always easy to judge scale from photographs: this large group of materials stands nearly 7 feet (2.1 metres) from the floor! Most of the materials that have been used in it are air-dried, but one or two of the fern fronds have been pressed. The scale of the arrangement could, of course, be reduced but at times a large group is needed and so I thought it would make useful reference for a book of this sort.

It would, though, be too overpowering and dark for the normal living room, I feel. For something "friendlier" in the same size I would suggest changing the materials and having light colours and pastel shades: try using delphinium (larkspur), achillea, echinops ritro, limonium (statice), bupleurum and pretty pale hydrangeas. The foliage materials could be those I have used for this arrangement: tilia (lime) and some of the same fern or bracken fronds (pteridium aquilinum and similar varieties).

PEDESTAL CONTAINERS

First, though, let me tell you about the container because I find this a very useful one to have. It is a semi-rectangular teak plinth with a panelled front, also in teak. Usefully, it has a built-in container: a zinc lining is set into the top. This water container is 9 inches (23 centimetres) deep, and provides plenty of space for stems. For this dried group, I have used one block of oasis sec, largely to steady the back stems. It is held in with 2-inch (5-centimetre) gauge netting over and round the sides of the oasis.

Before I describe how to make this arrangement, here are some general remarks. To lend fullness to the group, one or two stems on each side of the centre have been positioned leaning back slightly. A nice effect, but only possible if the pedestal is standing away from the background or is placed in the corner of a room. Something I would have liked very much to add to the arrangement would have been some large flower heads, positioned in the centre of the group. The many small seedheads I have used do not give the visual weight required and do not show up well, unless one stands close to them. The end result is "busy" rather than "clean cut". Two good teaching points, though, can be learnt from this group: first, always keep long stems on your materials when you want them for a large group, and secondly, try to ensure that you have a few well-placed large flowers or leaves to give a defined centre to your arrangement.

Now let me explain how this group was put together. Let's begin with the outline foliage. As there is a large bulk of material to go into the container, work as far to the back of it as you can with the outline flowers. Fix the tilia (lime) branch first for height, then on the left position the long arching acanthus and on the right another stem of lime with flower buds. Now place one or two similar stems, leaning backwards to give the all-round effect mentioned earlier and to help balance the container. The fronds of osmunda regalis (royal fern) may now be positioned: try to achieve a fan shape through the group. This variety may well need delicate handling. Now fix the three large fronds of cycas in place (one of these is the large brown compound leaf clearly

Dried Foliage on a Teak Pedestal

showing over the front of the pedestal). Now is the moment to fit in all the remaining curved acanthus flower stems: they carry the white residue of flowers at the tips of their stems. Next, position some heads of lunaria biennis (honesty), preferably those still carrying the seed and protective cover to the pods which keeps them green/brown rather than silver. The heads take up quite a bit of room so get them in before the arrangement becomes too full.

Now add some branches of buddleia (the cone-shaped seedheads are quite attractive), and seedheads of iris, lilium pyrenaicum, allium and malva moschata (mallow), bringing each through the group in sweeps. There is one stem of oenothera biennis (evening primrose) with a most attractive seedhead. The principle you are seeking is fluidity: try to get every stem to flow from the centre. Always ensure that different shapes and lengths are next to each other. It's important, too, to know when to stop: nothing is worse than an overcrowded arrangement!

Foliage and Seedheads in a Celadon Vase

This modern ceramic vase would fit into most homes. A suitable colour range would include off-white, grey, celadon as illustrated, brown and mat black. There are very few dried materials, I believe, that would not look good arranged in such a vase in one of these colours. Standing 18 inches (46 centimetres) tall, it does take up quite a large space, though, and requires stems of one-and-a-half to two times this height to give a good, balanced arrangement. For safety's sake, I would suggest that the bottom 12 inches (30 centimetres) be filled with dry sand or gravel, to provide a good sturdy base for the arrangement. Oasis or wire netting could then be positioned in the top 6 inches (15 centimetres) to hold the stems in position. As far as the choice of materials is concerned, the basic rule is that the lighter the materials used, the taller the stems, and the final arrangement, can be. "Light", in this context, doesn't just mean physically light, but also visually light: thin, slender, graceful. Both wild and cultivated (cereal) grasses are much lighter in this sense than are dried proteas, for example, though the physical weight of half-a-dozen specimens may be similar. My own opinion is that a vase of this sort is ideal for simple stems of grasses, seedheads and a few leaves as you see in the picture. Some flowers, though, could easily be worked into the arrangement to give some variety from time to time.

BALANCED ARRANGEMENTS IN A TALL VASE

An important point to remember with a vase of this shape is that materials with curved stems are essential for the sides of the arrangement if the overall effect is to be balanced and not too upright. These curved stems help link the rest of the materials to the container. A similar purpose is served by the leaves of magnolia and protea which have been put on double leg mounts (see page 56) and wired, to bring them out over the rim of the vase. Had this rim been left showing, it would give the impression of a hard dividing line between plant material and container; the arrangement then takes on what I call a "surprised look". Arrangement and container must always be linked together by stems of material to give a rounded, satisfying result.

The first materials I positioned were typha angustifolia (reedmace) leaves, iris, a seedhead of rumex (dock), and cimicifuga stems with their short, feathery flower heads. All of these help set the height of the arrangement. The width is set next with stipa calamagrostis grass and a digitalis (foxglove) seedhead. Position the paeonia suffruticosa (tree peony) pods at the centre of the group.

Having set the height and width of the arrangement, and fitted the more difficult items into the centre, you can now begin to fill in the outline using the rest of your materials. I have used black marsh grass, with its attractive feathery fronds of dark seedheads, sparganium simplex (simple bur-reed), with its spiky, bright green seed capsules that look like those of aesculus hippocastanum (horse chestnut or conker), sisyrinchium (which produces whorls of dark seed pods), hosta seedheads, cyperus alternifolius (umbrella grass), allium siculum and delphinium.

All of these materials have been air-dried except for the iris and reedmace leaves, which were pressed under a carpet. I have also used some pressed epimedium leaves. In the case of the iris leaves, you may want to help them stay firm by running thin cane up their backs, and holding it in position with oasis tape. This takes the place of the mid-rib not present in plants of this sort (monocotyledons).

TIPS AND TECHNIQUES

With a vase of these dimensions, the amount of open space you have in which to insert your materials is strictly limited, so choosing material with fairly thin stems is important. Work from the back rim to start with, and see that the stems go into the container without crossing over one another. (If they do this, you will be using more space in the neck of the vase than you have to.) As you position the taller materials at the back, allow one or two of the stems to lean slightly backwards: this will give the group more of an all-round effect. When you set in the two sides, position about three stems on each side to make two blocks of three stems. Each stem should be just a little different in length. Once these tall back and side points have been set, do not allow other materials to go out past them. They fix the outline of the group. As mentioned above, keep the stems neatly to the back of the oasis so that more stems can go in front. As you position materials in the centre, make sure that some of the stems come right out over the front of the vase.

Foliage and Seedheads in a Celadon Vase

Don't hesitate to do this, even if you fear that the end result will not be pleasing. You can, in fact, always allow an arrangement to come out of a vase to at least half the height of the arrangement, measured from the rim (see the side view diagram below).

Once the front point has been set, work back into the vase from this point, making each piece you put in just a little bit shorter than the previous one. If the longest piece had a 6 inch (15 centimetre) stem, for

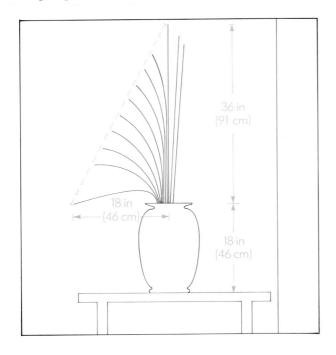

36 in
(91 cm)

18 in
(46 cm)

18 in
(46 cm)

example, then the next piece would have a 4½ inch (11 centimetre) stem, the next one a 3 inch (7 centimetres) stem, and then finally one deep in the centre of the arrangement with a 2 inch (5 centimetre) stem. Now work a section down through the centre of the arrangement, preparing and placing stems in a similar way, each one a little shorter than the last one, zigzagging them through the group, working again at an angle as you come lower. The side view of your arrangement should make a roughly triangular shape, with a gradual line from the tallest to the widest point (as indicated by the diagram, left). Look at each piece carefully as you put it into the vase: if, for instance, you have three allium heads of different sizes, try to grade them so that the largest one is positioned in the lowest point. (This is not essential, but it does add visual weight, which helps to balance the finished arrangement.)

These tips are not rules, of course: there are many ways of doing things, but I know from my own experience that if you make a plan in your mind based on the materials you have available, you will get a more pleasing effect. Do not crowd the vase. You may find that you do not want to use all your material. Because dried material does not have much, if any, foliage attached to its stems, one tends to have more filling-in between the major pieces to do, and it is easy, then, to get carried away and end with what I call a "stuffed" effect. Slipping one or two pieces of a fern frond through the bare stems at the base of your arrangement will often help considerably.

A Wild Flower Collection

This most attractive arrangement has been made exclusively from materials collected during a day's walking on the Sussex Downs in Southern England. The materials have therefore been provided by chance, rather than being chosen to fit a specific scheme, and I think it shows just how much can be done using a bare minimum of material and your imagination. Credit in this instance should go to my colleague Rosemary Minter, who both collected and arranged these gleanings.

One should always be hesitant about cutting wild specimens in case they should prove to be rare. Modern methods of farming and hedge-brushing have done away with many of our wild flowers, and

made the survival of many more look uncertain. But if you follow the guidelines below, you should come home with a suitable collection, having done no harm to the balance of nature.

If you come across a large patch of a particular species, or something that you know you have seen on numerous occasions in other locations, then you can always pick a number of stems without worry. If, though, you find anything unusual, particularly if it is growing in a small group or on its own, then leave it alone. If possible, take a photograph of it and identify it later, then you will know whether or not it's an endangered species. (Picking endangered species is illegal.)

A Wild Flower Collection

These materials have been arranged in an antique silver jewel box. It's a small item – the complete arrangement stands only 12 inches (30 centimetres) high – so you will not need a large amount of material to fill it. As I have said earlier, some of the pieces that one may find when browsing in antique shops make excellent containers for dried flower arrangements. The great advantage of dried materials is that they do not need containers which hold water. Slight imperfections can be covered up by the materials used in the arrangement.

DRYING AND ARRANGING

All the materials are positioned in a piece of close-fitting oasis sec, inserted into the jewel box. Most of the materials were at least partially dried on the plant: quite a common phenomenon during and after a spell of good weather. Any pieces requiring a little more drying were hung in a warm, dark cupboard to air-dry fully for a few days.

The first step in making the arrangement is to set the height and width with the fern or bracken fronds. In this small-scale arrangement everything should be positioned to radiate out from the centre point, and the bracken can be clearly seen to do this. Next, position more of the long stems between the fern fronds, and bring some of these out from the front of the container, too. Again, keep all of these radiating out from the centre of the arrangement. Finally, fill in the centre and margins with more seedheads and flower stems, taking care not to crowd the arrangement. With small-scale work like this, delicacy is all.

As the materials for this arrangement were the casual gleanings of a day's country walking, it is unlikely that you'll be able to reproduce them exactly! But of course the point of this arrangement is to show how it's possible to use whatever is to hand and still produce something special and memorable. For the record, though, here are some of the varieties that the keen botanist will be able to spot in the picture: side shoots of rumex (dock) with seedheads, a number of flowering ericaceae (heathers), plantago media (plantain) seedheads, achillea millefolium (white yarrow), briza media (quaking grass), small seedheads of scabiosa columbaria (scabious), and two different members of the labiatae family, both with characteristically square stems. Melissa officinalis (balm), stachys officinalis (betony) and ballota nigra (black horehound) can also be seen.

One or two items with weak stems have been wired to give support (see page 56), but this has been kept to a minimum. Never wire more material than you need to because wired items can take on a stiff appearance which detracts from the free and natural ideal that one should seek in all arrangements. I shall always remember Constance Spry's words on the subject: "The wiring of flowers is for floristry and there it should stay." She never allowed pupils to wire flowers in arrangements.

A Small Arrangement for the Professional Desk

This elegant arrangement for a desk top is small, and does not take up too much vital space on the work surface. Yet it provides the touch of colour so often missing from a sober professional environment. The colouring of the container's stand links up with the inkwell tops and the gilt work on the leather desk top: these details are all points worth considering when making a permanent arrangement to fit the decor of a particular room. The advantage of an arrangement using dried materials is that it will last over a long period – but this could become a disadvantage if the arrangement is out of harmony with its setting in any way.

I always enjoy working with this container: it seems to display material so elegantly. It is very shallow, though, and shallow containers can pose problems when you try to fix materials into them firmly. I will discuss this further below.

It is made up of a little metal stand with two dolphins at its base. I found this in a box of assorted "antiques" in a London junk shop, and I believe it used to be part of an old ink stand. The top was missing so I found a small flat shell to rest on it. This just fits when laid across the metal framework. I secure it firmly with two cross-pieces of wire because, for obvious reasons, this must not move. This, I think, illustrates my earlier comments on how something that looked initially unpromising can soon be put to good use. As a container, it would have very limited use with fresh material, but I have found it excellent with dried material and have used it many times.

In the shell, I have placed a piece of oasis sec about $3 \times 1 \times 1$ inches ($7.5 \times 2.5 \times 2.5$ centimetres). This needs fixing with care: I use a blob of oasis fix in the base of the shell to keep it firm. The positioning medium must always be rigid before you start arranging flowers, or disaster could ensue later. Overall, the container has a solid base and is light at the top so there is no fear of it falling over.

POSITIONING THE MATERIALS

For this arrangement, as for the previous one and for small arrangements in general, all the stems radiate out from a centre point. The first thing to do is to set a background for the stems. For this I have used three side-fronds of osmunda regalis (royal fern) – just enough to make a light background for the flowers. They were placed at the back of the small piece of oasis and made to flow from the centre point. I then put in some pieces of broken hydrangea head deep down in the arrangement to cover the mechanics. These, too, provide a sort of background to the main stems, and have simply been pinned to the oasis. Together with these pieces of broken hydrangea are a few heads of

A Small Arrangement for the Professional Desk

white achillea (yarrow). These serve the same purpose. Then I set the height and width with lavandula spica (old English lavender) and limonium suworowii (statice). With height, width and background materials all in place, it was now time to fit in the important stems: those that provide the focal points of the arrangement. In this case, I have used two heads of eryngium grandiflorum (sea holly): one of my favourite dried materials. Then a few stems of heli-

chrysum were added. These were the only materials I had to wire before use, as their stems were simply not strong enough to go into the oasis. They have to be tucked in deep in the arrangement to hide these false stems. The rest of the material was added in groups, positioned through the arrangement. You will see that the lavender and statice go from side to side, and I have positioned some baby eryngium planum in curves over the front right and up to the top left. The effect you should be seeking is not that of blocks of material, but of similar stems lightly grouped together: this is always better than having them spotted about an arrangement. No two adjacent stems should be the same length. Get some flowers in low down, in the middle of the arrangement, to add visual weight to the centre of the vase. All the stems, as I stressed earlier, should flow from the central point. Don't forget to make use of naturally curved

material to come over the front and sides of the vase to hide the rim of the container and so avoid that hard look that so often mars arrangements. Stems used in this way will also help link the decoration to its immediate environment. The remaining materials I have used were limonium sinuatum and seedheads of papaver (poppy). All were air-dried, with the exception of the osmunda fronds, which were pressed between sheets of newspaper positioned under a carpet.

A Flower Cone

This spectacular and highly coloured group would be ideal standing in an alcove or somewhere there is plenty of room to show it off well. It has been constructed in an antique bronze Warwick urn on a small plinth. The sort of interior environment it suggests to me is one rich with dark wood furniture; it would be ideal seen against a background of wood panelling. Yet such an arrangement could be equally well made in a modern wooden tub or plastic flower pot; it would then be ideal for a contemporary interior. The two important points to remember about the arrangement are that it stands, at present, about 4 feet (1.22 metres) high, so it will need plenty of room to be properly appreciated, and that the base must be heavy enough to support the arrangement safely.

The joy of these cones is that they can be made in any size you wish, though of course the size of the materials should be in proportion to the finished arrangement. This means, in effect, that little versions are more exacting to make than large versions, as the choice of materials is limited and the positioning work very finicky. The size we have photographed is relatively easy to do, because there is a wealth of material available to go into it.

CONSTRUCTING A CONE
The basic design for all sizes of cone is the same. A piece of wire netting is cut so that when the two ends are joined together it will form a cone shape. The inside of this is tightly packed with teased-out sphagnum moss, and at the same time a wooden pole is inserted in the middle of the cone, reaching to the top and extending out below the bottom. This pole is then positioned in soil in the pot or urn in which the cone sits, to keep the whole construction steady. The cone is then ready to have materials inserted into it.

Here are some dimensions to help you get an idea of the proportions required. A small one would be made with small mesh (1-inch or 2.5-centimetre) wire netting, forming a cone 12 inches (30 centimetres) high and 5 inches (12.5 centimetres) wide at the base. It's best to cut out a paper template first to check that you have the correct shape before cutting out the wire. Remember that you'll need some overlap to join the ends up effectively. A cone of the size photographed would need to be 20 inches (51 centimetres) wide at the base. As you pack the teased-out moss, insert the stake which will support the centre and go into the soil in the tub, steadying the whole structure: this could be a piece of old broom handle or strong dowelling rod. (For a small cone you can, of course, use a ready-made oasis sec or polystyrene cone, but these are light and somewhat insecure, I feel.)

DECORATING THE CONE
When making a permanent decoration using dried materials, everything should be mounted on double leg mounts. This will give the materials a much firmer hold on the moss and wire. Instructions on making both single and double leg mounts are given on page 56: it's a good idea to do this work first.

Position the green background material first. If you use a variety of materials, as I have done here, then see that these materials are evenly spread out around the cone. You will see, in the photograph, laurus (bay), cupressus (cypress) and juniperus (juniper). I would suggest that you make up a number of pieces of each material beforehand, placing each type separately in seed boxes or small buckets. Then work systematically, taking one from each box in rotation, as you work from the top down to the wider base. For a really elegant look, try to ensure that the pieces at

A Flower Cone

the top are just a little smaller than those at the bottom, to get a more even finish to the whole cone. Set the cone at a good working height: press the double legs right into the moss, then tilt the mount slightly to grip closely to the cone. You must step back and check frequently that you are respecting the shape of the cone. Once you have a fair covering of different greens, wire up the flowers, fruits, nuts and berries, using double leg mounts. Again, keep each variety in separate sections and work through in the same way, to the bottom, adding to the framework.

The varieties I have used include helichrysum bracteatum, achillea eupatorium, tassels of garrya elliptica and heads of physalis alkekengi (Chinese lanterns), dried flower heads of humulus lupus (hops) and seedheads of clematis vitalba (old man's beard). I have also used cones of pinus sylvestris (Scots pine) and the residual bases of cedrus deodara cones. The final addition was of clusters of castanea sativa (sweet chestnut) as they emerge from their spiny seed cases.

If you intend to place your cone standing in an alcove or positioned in the corner of the room, you will only need to cover three-quarters of the surface with materials, as the rest will not show. Cover the bare surface at the back with a strip of polythene, pinned on neatly to keep any bits of moss from falling out as the cone becomes old and dry.

The rim of the cone at the base should be well filled out. The stems positioned there should be slightly larger than the rest, and you should finish off the arrangement in its final resting place, making sure that the bottom materials cover the rim of the urn or vase.

A Pomander Tree

This is something a little different. It came about when a discussion started on how one could use pomanders – those highly scented, clove-covered oranges which used to be so popular years ago and are now back in vogue – as a decoration. By having four or five together, one would really be able to enjoy their spicy scent, much as one enjoys potpourri. On looking through a collection of other materials I came across a number of shadow leaves (skeletonized magnolia leaves) and then the idea suddenly came to me. They could hang from a small tree, together with these leaves. The tree in this instance is in fact made from some old tree roots that have been washed and bleached by the constant movement of water lapping against them. They may be found at the edge of Scottish lochs in this form. If a trip to Scotland is not possible, then one may also purchase roots which have been sand-blasted to give them a smooth finish.

PREPARING THE MATERIALS

In this arrangement I have used two pieces of pine root wired together, and set them in an old clay pot. The terracotta colouring blends well with the brown of the cloves and the neutral, translucent straw-brown of the leaves.

The skeletonized magnolia leaves are produced in Italy and exported worldwide: your local florist should be able to obtain them for you. It is the vein network, denuded of all the spongy cell tissue, that makes the light, papery skeleton of each leaf. Check over the leaves in the packet: they won't all be perfect (they aren't in nature, either): only use the best. You could also try making them yourself, though I feel duty bound to warn you that this is not easy. Instructions are given on the opposite page.

Each magnolia leaf should then be wired before being attached to the tree. I have to admit, though, that I have cheated here in using a new piece of equipment that I have recently been introduced to: the glue gun. It did an excellent job with these leaves. If you use one, work over paper or a covered surface as spots of glue tend to drop from time to time.

If you don't wish to glue these leaves to the branches, then mount them, using double leg mounts (see page 56), on silver wires covered with gutta-percha. This covered wire is then twisted round the stem of the tree and in turn guttared to finish off.

When making the pomanders, I find it best to use medium-sized oranges with thick skins: the thin skinned ones do not hold the cloves so well. Divide the fruit into four sections, and spike each section with cloves in neat rows, leaving four channels for the ribbon that holds the fruit to fit into. (A good tip is to make a small hole with a toothpick before pushing the clove into the skin: this makes the job much easier.) Quarter-inch (0.6 centimetre) baby ribbon is normally wide enough, especially if it has a picot edge like that used in the photograph.

Attach the leaves first, stepping back from time to time to check that you are achieving a balanced appearance. When you have positioned the leaves to

A Pomander Tree

your satisfaction, attach the pomanders to the tree at strategic places, again checking carefully that balance hasn't been lost. An odd number of pomanders will give a more pleasing result than an even number when working with a small-scale arrangement. Three or five pomanders are better than four which, however arranged, tend to make a square effect. Finally, the surface of the flower pot is finished by filling it up with gravel and laying some bleached pine cones on the surface.

Once complete, you will have to find the right background to set the tree against: something plain and dark is best. The shadow leaves tend to "disappear" when positioned against a light coloured fabric or paper. A final point worth remembering is that the atmosphere must be kept dry when using skeletonized leaves, as they will go limp if there's any dampness in the air. A bathroom or unheated sun lounge would be a bad environment for the tree, whereas a warm dry bedroom would be ideal.

POMANDERS

Constance Spry was very fond of pomanders and I remember how, back in the 1950s, we used to make them for sale each winter. In *A Constance Spry Anthology* (J.M. Dent, 1953) she says:

> Perhaps one of the nicest ways of perfuming a room is by having in it a bowl of pomanders. The use of these dates back to those early days when the streets of London were so malodorous that fashionable ladies and dandies carried them about so that their noses need not be too roughly assailed. The name derives from the French *pomme d'ambre* – "apple of amber" – and used to be a ball made of such perfume as ambergris or musk which was carried in a perforated case, sometimes made of gold or silver and ornamented with jewels.

In London's British Museum there is a Spanish example set with emeralds, dating from the sixteenth century and found in the mud of the river Thames.

Nowadays, of course, pomanders denote the more mundane clove-stuck oranges described opposite. Many people find Seville or bitter oranges superior to ordinary oranges for pomanders, and this is worth remembering if you are making yours early in the year. Another tip is to put the orange into a cool oven to dry after it has been stuck with the cloves. You'd think that after a spell of normal exposure in a warm room, the orange would decay but this does not happen if the pomander is properly made. Sometimes pomanders made in this way, once dried, are pounded up and added to potpourris.

USING SWEET-SMELLING MATERIALS

Many types of potpourri are available today, but they vary a great deal in quality. The really good ones are expensive to make but should last a great deal longer. The moist varieties are probably best for scenting rooms, since dry ones need stirring all the time to give off their scent. I suggest you try Constance Spry's own potpourri, recipe given on page 42. I have always found it to be really long-lasting.

In Constance Spry's *Garden Notebook* (J.M. Dent, 1940) I have found these comments on potpourris:

> Thinking ahead for sweet scents in the house in winter we begin to harvest rose petals, sweet smelling herbs or any fragrant flowers that become available. In gathering rose petals I find it a good plan to spread them out for an hour or two on sheets to allow to dry a little and then I pack them into deep jars with salt, a handful of rough salt to every handful of roses. Sometimes the salt will draw out a thick brown juice from the petals and unless mould appears this liquid is valuable, but it is as well to dry up the mixture with powdered orris root.
>
> If, however, the petals remain reasonably dry, the orris root may wait until the time comes for mixing the whole into potpourri. We gather leaves of mint, thyme, lemon verbena, sweet geranium and flowers of lavender, white jasmine, scotch marigolds and sweet violets. All are dried a little before being put away in readiness for the final making into potpourri which we do in October.

How to Skeletonize Leaves

This was a popular pastime in the nineteenth century. Follow this method, choosing strong leaves as your material. Magnolia is the best leaf for this, but you might also like to try prunus laurocerasus (common laurel), camellia and ficus elastica (India-rubber plant).

1 Add a teaspoonful (5 ml) of washing soda to 2 pints (1.2 litres) of water, then heat this solution to boiling point. Add the leaves, and simmer them gently in the water for 30 minutes. Cool the leaves in cold water.

2 Remove the leaves from the water and lay gently on a piece of paper on a flat surface.

3 Very carefully scrape off all the green leaf tissue, using the back of a knife, but do not split or tear the leaf framework.

4 Place the leaves in a very weak bleach solution for about 1 hour.

5 Rinse the leaves in clean cold water. Pat the leaves dry very carefully, then press them lightly between sheets of blotting paper.

6 Wire the leaves, using double leg mounts (page 56), when dry. If some of the leaves are weak and soft, wire them with a loop of thin gauge florist's wire at the back for additional support.

A Floral Potpourri Basket

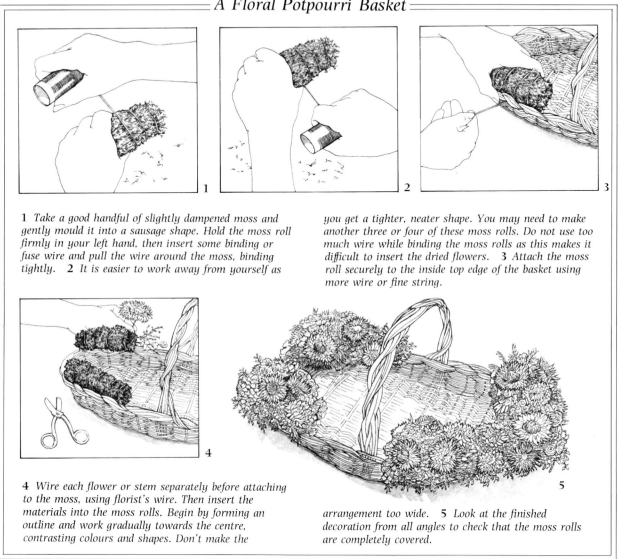

1 Take a good handful of slightly dampened moss and gently mould it into a sausage shape. Hold the moss roll firmly in your left hand, then insert some binding or fuse wire and pull the wire around the moss, binding tightly. **2** It is easier to work away from yourself as you get a tighter, neater shape. You may need to make another three or four of these moss rolls. Do not use too much wire while binding the moss rolls as this makes it difficult to insert the dried flowers. **3** Attach the moss roll securely to the inside top edge of the basket using more wire or fine string.

4 Wire each flower or stem separately before attaching to the moss, using florist's wire. Then insert the materials into the moss rolls. Begin by forming an outline and work gradually towards the centre, contrasting colours and shapes. Don't make the arrangement too wide. **5** Look at the finished decoration from all angles to check that the moss rolls are completely covered.

WICKERWORK FOR COLOUR CONTRAST

A basket is an ideal container for potpourri as its wide shape allows the pleasing petal odours to circulate freely, while the light colour of wicker makes a suitable contrast to the multicoloured contents. But to make it still more decorative, add some dried flowers in clusters on the rim of the basket.

Choose a low-sided basket – it may be round, oblong or rectangular but it does need to have a wide exposed area to show off the potpourri. (You may either buy potpourri ready-made or make your own: Constance Spry's recipe is given on page 42.) The colours of potpourri are as enjoyable as its scent: try for either a group that includes pink, red, mauve and blue colours, or one with petals in golden yellow, brown and rust. But there are no rules here: just get a pleasing colour scheme to suit your house. Try to include some whole flowers or parts of flowers in the mixture, too. You may, of course, use containers other than baskets to hold potpourri, but you will

A Floral Potpourri Basket

have difficulty in adding the extra floral decoration as we have done here.

For step-by-step instructions as to how to make the flower decoration, see opposite. The flowers used are a selection of different species of helichrysum and limonium (statice). All have been air-dried. The helichrysum has been mounted on double leg mounts, (see page 56) whereas the statice is simply wired on to short single leg mounts before being inserted into the moss. A wide variety of different

materials may be used in the sprays – just wire up in the ordinary way and then position in the moss.

One important point to remember, though, when selecting and mounting materials to form the floral decoration for the basket is that they shouldn't be too big, or both the sight and smell of the potpourri will be obscured. Small, delicate shapes and bright colours (the statice is ideal here) are what you're looking for: save any big, impressive heads you may have to form the centrepiece of a separate decoration.

Constance Spry's Potpourri Recipe

1 lb (450g) rough salt
3 oz (75g) saltpetre
a large bucketful of rose petals dried for a few hours in
    the sun
1 oz (25g) each of ground cinnamon, allspice, cloves
    and nutmeg
1 oz (25g) ground storax
4 oz (100g) powdered orris root
juice and chopped rind of 3 lemons
½ fl oz (15 ml) each of bergamot oil, spirit of lavender,
    geranium oil and lemon essence

Mix the salt with the saltpetre. Put some of the rose petals into a jar, sprinkling each handful of petals with some of the salt mixture. In a second jar, mix the spices together. Add the storax and powdered orris root. Mix all the ingredients well together, then add the lemon juice and rind with the remaining oils and liquids. Mix together the powders, liquids and the salted rose petals in the bottom of one jar.

You now have the nucleus of your potpourri. To this mixture you may add, at any stage during the summer season, more rose petals, either fresh, dried or treated with salt, but each time you make an addition, the mixture should be well stirred.

Later in the year, the following leaves may be added, but all should be dried first: sweet geranium, sweet verbena, bergamot and sweet bay. The flowers of lavender and leaves of rosemary, both stripped from their stems, will make another good addition. Some people also like to add cedarwood chips and coriander seed. Personal favourites of mine are dried mint and thyme, though additions like these are a matter of taste.

When the whole mixture is complete and well mixed you can, if you like, add two or three glasses of brandy. If the potpourri is too moist add some powdered orris root; if too dry, add some salt.

During all the time that the potpourri is being made – from the very first mixing of the rose petals with the salt and saltpetre until the final leaves and flowers are put in – it should be kept tightly covered. This mixture will last almost indefinitely and may be added to freshly gathered materials which should not be dried first. It will only remain really effective in the house as long as it isn't allowed to dry out.

A Decorative Flower Ball

This large flower ball is made by inserting dried flower materials into a 6 inch (15 centimetre) oasis sec sphere. It could also have been made by forming a sphere of well teased-out damp moss and binding this together with string or wire, but the oasis sec is much cleaner and easier to use. The finished ball will also be considerably lighter if made with oasis: an important point if, as we have done, you wish to hang the ball from the ceiling with ribbon.

All the pieces of flower material used for this arrangement have first been cut into lengths of 2–3 inches (5–7.5 centimetres). Do not, though, make all the pieces the same length because this will give a very heavy and less interesting finish to the work. The length of the various pieces of material should differ by as much as 1 inch (2.5 centimetres). Flower materials that have naturally stiff stems – such as limonium (statice), rosa (rose) or lavandula (lavender) – may simply be stuck into the oasis, while the others are mounted on double leg mounts. (If you are using moss you will find that nearly everything has to be mounted.)

Before you begin to insert the flower materials, though, take a 10-inch (25-centimetre) length of wire and cover it with gutta-percha or crepe paper. Push this wire right through the sphere, making a loop on the end. Pull the wire back into the oasis so that you have a good round loop (this will form the top of the sphere, and the ribbon for hanging the sphere will thread through this) then tuck the other end of the wire into the oasis to hold the loop firm.

A Decorative Flower Ball

42

DECORATING THE SPHERE

Set up the sphere by standing it in a basin or flowerpot with the loop at the top: it will look like an egg in an eggcup. Begin to insert the pieces of dried material, stepping back from time to time to ensure an even finish. In this arrangement we have used limonium (statice) in two kinds (limonium sinuatum and limonium latifolium) and in different colours; alchemilla; santolina; sprays of lavandula (lavender) and some helichrysum flowers. Mix them well in the arrange-ment, getting different lengths next to each other. Work right down to the edge of the basin or flowerpot in which the oasis is standing. Keep turning the sphere as you add the materials, to make sure that you get an even shape. When all of the exposed area of the sphere is completed, hold by the loop, turn the sphere upside down and tuck in the remaining pieces to complete the arrangement.

Finish off by drawing a good ribbon through the loop and securing it with some bows.

A Scented Lavender Tree

This lavender tree – like the Flower Ball on the previous pages – is really a form of indoor topiary. (Another example of this is the Flower Cone on pages 36–37.) This type of work is attractive and not too difficult to make. A lavender tree serves two purposes: it provides a pretty decoration, but it also scents the room at the same time. Lavender and similar trees can be made in varying sizes to suit different interiors and occasions. The length of the lavender tree stem is the controlling factor, together with the size of tub that you would like to set the tree in. Two alternatives would be to make a smaller pair of decorations for a mantelpiece or sideboard, or a single small decoration for a table or desk.

MAKING THE TREE

The same principle operates for the construction of any of these trees, regardless of size, so I will describe the basic design. First select a display tub and the correct size flowerpot to fit it, remembering that the size you choose will to some extent dictate the size and height of the stem, and the size of the ball of moss or oasis which goes on top of the pole. The length of the pole, as a rough guideline, should be no more than five times the diameter of the flowerpot. In the photograph the following sizes have been used: in a $3\frac{1}{2}$-inch (9-centimetre) flowerpot (known as a stan-dard 60 pot) we have set a 15-inch (38-centimetre) length of $\frac{1}{4}$-inch (0.6-centimetre) dowelling. (Bamboo cane of similar dimensions could also be used.) The oasis sphere positioned on top of the pole is 3 inches (7.6 centimetres) in diameter.

The dowelling should first be covered in a suitable fabric – in this case a moss-green hessian has been used, but a similarly coloured length of ribbon would also look attractive. Stand the pole upright and set it in the flowerpot. This can be done in any way you wish: I have used a quick drying cement for a secure finish, but carefully positioned wedges would do. If using any form of cement, remember to line the pot first with newspaper: this will prevent the pot crack-ing when the cement expands as it dries out. Check carefully, with a spirit level if possible, that the stem is upright. The pole may look only fractionally off a true vertical at this stage, but when the arrangement is finished, the problem will appear much worse.

If you are using an oasis sphere to mount the flower material on, you'll find that this presses on to the wooden pole quite easily. If you're using a ball of moss, then the first thing to do is to fix two nails on to either side of the pole near the top. These nails will provide something for the pieces of sphagnum moss to grip on. Make sure that the ball is round by stepping back to check your work from time to time: if it is not then the finished arrangement will look strange. Trim the moss well with scissors to make a neat sphere.

ATTACHING THE FLOWER MATERIALS

Now you can begin work on the arrangement itself. First pin on the grey lichen moss (also known as reindeer moss), again taking great care to keep the overall shape round. Cut the stems of flower heads of echinops ritro (globe thistle) down to about 1 inch (2.5 centimetres), and then mount each head on double leg mounts (see page 56). Set these heads into the moss, ensuring that they are evenly distributed on all sides of the sphere, and that plenty of space is left between each large head. You may find that you are able to stick the lavandula (lavender) heads straight into the sphere, but if they are too flimsy and this is

A Scented Lavender Tree

not possible, mount them up into small bunches. Each bunch should contain no more than 3–5 stems. Set these into the sphere, stepping back continually to check from a distance for a well-balanced result. Try to ensure that either the single stems of lavender or the small groups are all of different lengths. This is very important for a really pleasing result. Finally, finish the arrangement with bows or ribbon ends of the same material that you have used to bind the wooden or bamboo pole. Then cover the base of the pot with more grey lichen moss or bun moss, positioning it to give an attractive finish.

VARIATIONS ON THE THEME

There are, of course, endless variations to be created on the theme of "indoor trees", like this example made using lavender. As mentioned above, smaller versions for the mantelpiece or shelf could be produced without much difficulty, though you will need to find small, delicate materials to use in these to preserve their proportions. For a special occasion such as a big summer party or wedding, large trees of limonium (statice) can be very attractive. These may be made up to 4 feet (1.2 metres) high, and look very handsome standing at the entrance of a house or marquee. Broom sticks make useful stems, fixed into clay flower pots the size of large buckets. The principles for arranging the materials are identical to those described above: these are, in fact, fairly simple and straightforward decorations for the practiced arranger, and it is always easier to make a large tree than a very small one, in which a lot of detailed work is necessary. Remember, though, that a pole set in concrete in a clay pot will be very heavy: you may, therefore, want to make the arrangement in the position in which it is needed!

—— A Strawberry Pot of Herbs ——

This attractive clay pot, with a wide range of culinary herbs arranged in it, makes an excellent decoration for a kitchen, especially an open-plan kitchen where there is perhaps a dining area which needs some form of decoration. It's a dual-purpose arrangement, as it contains all the dried herbs you need to use for day-to-day cookery, while at the same time providing the room with visual interest. Herbs are really most attractive plants, and it is neglectful not to make something of this kind with them, I feel. The arrangement also illustrates another point that I cannot reiterate often enough: a decoration must always be right for the room you have it in.

A CONTAINER FOR THE KITCHEN

Strawberry pots have been popular items for use in the garden for many years. Today they come in different styles, and are made in various materials: I have seen both metal and plastic examples. There is nothing nicer, though, than genuine clay pottery. They can also be bought set in a hanging basket, which may suit a smaller kitchen, but for choice I would always go for the old style which is, after all, available in many sizes. Do not try to use one which is too large, as the herbs you cook with less frequently may become very dry and fall, spoiling the arrangement. It is better to keep rearranging a smaller pot with freshly dried herbs. The arrangement can then be tidied up every two weeks or so.

The size we have used here, which is the maximum size I would suggest you use, can be gauged from the basket of eggs at the side. The pot itself is about 10 inches (25 centimetres) high, and has six pockets for holding the herbs, plus space for a large bunch at the top. If room permits, you may arrange the pot as an all-round group, but my own feeling is that in a kitchen, where one always seems to be short of space, it will be a facing arrangement that is needed, with the top, front and side pockets utilized.

All the herbs have been air-dried, each stem being cleaned of foliage to about a quarter of its total length, and then made into little bunches. By keeping these bunches small you ensure that they'll be used and replaced quickly, which will help keep the arrangement tidy. Any leaves taken from the base of each stem need not be wasted, of course. If you have no immediate use for them, bag them up and freeze them until required. Most herbs are very easy to air-dry, and some – like thymus (thyme) – almost seem to grow ready-dried. If you have room in your airing cupboard, drying time will be accelerated, which helps preserve the flavour of the herbs.

PREPARING THE POT

The preparation of the strawberry pot for holding the herbs is comparatively simple. Decide first whether you want little bunches or individual stems in the pockets because whichever alternative you choose will demand a slightly different approach.

If you decide on individual stems (which will make the decoration slower to complete but perhaps quicker to use in your cooking), you will need to wedge a small piece of oasis in each pocket. Ordinary oasis is better than oasis sec for this purpose. If you make up little bunches, then nothing is necessary in the pockets – each bunch can simply be tucked in. (If you find the pockets a little large, just put a ball of wire netting into the pocket: this will provide support for the bunch.)

Now pack the centre of the pot firmly with tissue paper, leaving enough room in the top of the pot to hold a fairly large piece of oasis: you will probably use a third to half of a brick. The oasis should extend about 1 inch (2.5 centimetres) above the rim so that you can tuck stems in from the side as usual to stop the very upright, "surprised" look. For extra support, a piece of 2-inch (5-centimetre) gauge wire netting could be fixed over the top rim of the pot.

ARRANGING THE HERBS

To arrange the herbs, treat them just as you would do ordinary flower stems. Set the height first at the centre back, using your tallest herbs, then set the width with the side pieces. Try to work in groups, bringing these specimens down and through the arrangement. Fix some largish stems fairly early on (in our picture we have used helichrysum angustifolium, the curry plant) and then gradually fill in with interesting shape and colour, allowing variation in stem length to avoid a stuffed, flat look. You will, no doubt, be able to spot your favourite herbs: thymus (thyme), monarda (bergamot), salvia (sage), mentha (mint), rosmarinus (rosemary) and laurus (bay). After you have completed inserting the stems into the top of the pot, fill in the side pockets with individual stems or groups of stems. You will see from the photograph that herbs have been grouped together in different pockets: thyme in one, sage in another, and so on. This will make for convenience, as well as providing an attractive effect.

Another nice idea for the kitchen is the vegetable swag, illustrated and described on pages 94–95. Something else to look out for in older kitchens is an old-fashioned tripod pot stand. These make excellent vase stands, and another alternative use for them is in supporting a bowl of cut dried herbs – out of the way, yet still serving as a decoration.

A Strawberry Pot of Herbs

Dried Wild Flowers from Southern Africa

In this contemporary marble vase standing on a matching pink marble plinth, I have arranged a group of dried wild flowers from Southern Africa. All of the flowers come from the Cape Province, where some of the world's most beautiful species grow in abundance. Most are in their natural form; those that have a pink tone have been slightly coloured. As this colouring is very delicate it does not make them look too unnatural, and it certainly suits the background colour of the room. Brightly dyed varieties, on the other hand, should always be avoided. Careful selection of materials before you buy them will generally reward you with soft and subtle tones in dried materials, as in fresh.

WORKING WITH MARBLE

I have chosen a modern but very pleasing tazza-shaped container to use for this arrangement. I bought it many years ago to sell in one of the flower shops that the Constance Spry School worked with; when I found how good it was to use, I changed my plans and withdrew it from the selection of vases we had for sale! I felt straight away that it was an easy vase to use and my colleagues, I know, feel the same way. It has proved a most useful shape for all our needs. But of course even the finest vase must suit the room that the arrangement is intended for, or the whole effect will be lost. Here it stands on a pedestal in a well-proportioned room with high ceilings, giving the arrangement plenty of light and height. The pleasant salmon room colouring provides a quiet and harmonious background for these beautiful plants.

All of the materials are held in the 4-inch (10-centimetre) deep bowl of the carved marble vase. I lined the bowl with brown paper first, to stop the layers of wire netting scratching its polished surface. Then I positioned the wire netting, and inside that a small block of oasis sec to steady the extra long stems of leucodendron rubrum foliage, which I have used for height at the centre back and the two widest points (it was the longest material available in the bunch). There is no doubt in my mind that this group has a slightly "surprised" look to it, brought about by all the very stiff and straight-stemmed materials used. The protea, for instance, are magnificent specimens, but perhaps because of this they are on very straight, thick stems. Unfortunately there were no materials available with curved stems. I would have dearly liked to add some to this group to soften and balance it. Still, perhaps the group makes up in drama for what it lacks in balance and classicism.

The dark-centred protea are those of protea nerifolia, and the pink-pointed ones are protea repens. The flat heads, deep down in the centre of the vase, are those of helipterum eximium. On the left-hand side are one or two stems of brunia albiflora, while the wispy pieces on the right-hand side are stoebe fusca (known locally as slangbos) in a natural and artificially coloured pale pink form. Just to the right of the central stem of foliage is some leucodendron nervosum. Deep in the centre of the arrangement are two little daisy-type flowers called helipterum crispum. On longer stems with larch-like cones in the upper and lower left-hand side of the arrangement is leucodendron xanthocornus (salignam).

USING THE MATERIALS

I followed my usual method of approach in arranging these stems, beginning with the height and width, then setting large and imposing materials well out at the front. (Nearly all of the materials here, of course, are both large and imposing; the problem, if anything, was to find enough small materials to provide a contrast to the very showy heads.) From this point I worked back into the vase centre. Having then, in effect, set all the outlines, I was now free to work on filling in with the rest of the materials. Using more of the large proteas, I then brought the top flowers down in stages to the lowest point, working at an angle all the time to try to get flowing lines into the finished result. The materials were grouped together, species by species, but taking care to position no two heads of the same size next to each other. This is particularly important when, as here, the stems are all very stiff and straight, as this will be the only way in which you can get a sense of variety and movement into the arrangement. In this respect, too, it is very important to make sure that the outlines are broken and uneven.

This vase would lend itself to arrangements incorporating a wide variety of materials. Mixed foliages, for example, would look excellent in it, as would a group of mixed summer garden flowers, such as kniphofia, salpiglossis and atriplex, with dahlia and rosa for centre weight. For those who have my

Dried Wild Flowers from Southern Africa

previous book *The Constance Spry Book of Flower Arranging* (Sundial Publications, 1979, and Octopus Books, 1985) an arrangement like this can be seen on page 95, completed by my colleague Fred Wilkinson. You'll see there the flowing lines and sense of freedom and movement I would so liked to have had in this arrangement.

All of the dried materials used in the arrangement photographed here would be very long-lasting. Depending, of course, on the amount the room is used,

and whether or not there are smokers in the family or an open fire in the room, a quick dusting with a light feathered duster should clean off any dry dirt. For stickier, heavier dirt, I have washed substantial dried stems such as these in warm soapy water from time to time and quickly hung them up to dry and this has been successful. Even if this apparently rather drastic treatment doesn't work, when it's a question of otherwise throwing the stems away – you have nothing to lose!

A Basket of Australian Wild Flowers

It is not often that I have the chance of arranging Australian wild flowers. These were given to me especially for use in this book, and I found that they went very well together against a pleasing wooden background. I have always wanted to visit Australia to see its wild flowers, and if this is a taste of what is to come, then I cannot wait before I am off!

A PLEA FOR UNIFORM NAMES
Because of the great interest now taken throughout the world in dried flowers, many more are being exported and imported everywhere than was the case even five years ago. Due to increasing demand, movements of dried (and even fresh) flowers on a global scale now regularly take place. This can only be a good thing for those of us who love to buy and arrange flowers, and yet there is a problem becoming increasingly apparent in respect of this trade that I'd like to mention here. This problem is that in many cases the imported and exported materials go by descriptive names rather than their true botanical name, so they are often difficult to trace and describe correctly. The common or descriptive names themselves often vary considerably from one part of the world to another: a species may be known by one name in a supplier's catalogue and have an entirely different name in its country of origin (neither name bearing any resemblance to the true botanical name). I have certainly encountered immense difficulties in trying to obtain the correct botanical names for materials used in this and other arrangements.

Thank goodness, though, we do get so many different species available nowadays: it makes life much more interesting, whether these be properly named or otherwise. On the question of using "exotic" materials in general, I would say that you should, if possible, try to use materials from your own country first and foremost (they will always, in some way, look best at home), but when nothing of the right sort is available, or you simply feel like a change, then try materials from other countries and climates. It is human nature, after all, to want something lovely that someone else has got!

BOOK LEAVES, KANGAROO PAWS AND SIGNPOSTS
For this rather straightforward arrangement of the unusual and exotic, standing against a pleasing wooden background, I have chosen another basket: this time it's a round one with a very high handle, positioned in such a way that the flowers are all able to flow through the handle. All of the materials have been arranged in a small piece of oasis sec with netting fitted over the top. This is easily fixed because the basket has a very good zinc lining with small loops attached into which I have bent ears of the netting.

The first stem that goes in begins the process of fixing the height and width of the arrangement. For this purpose, I have used some stems of daviesia cordata (book leaf shrub). Setting the width on the left are hakea nut pods. The large flower heads are the next to be positioned, and here I have used the extraordinary spiny ball-like blooms of banksia baxteri, with the rather more elongated banksia occidentalis providing interest at the lower right-hand corner of the arrangement. Other varieties I have used include some stems of anigozanthus (known as kangaroo paw). The fascinating foliage with a saw-like leaf edge is called templetonia. On the right-hand side is some dryandra quercefolia. The sprays deep in the centre are verticorda brownei, while the white sprays higher up in the arrangement belong to lysinema ciliatum (known as curry rice). Exordia is tucked in at the bottom left-hand side. The pale, long-toothed "signpost" leaves are actually part of the leaf bases of kingia australis (djingarra). All these, I think you'll agree, make a memorable show.

Dried Material in a Rectangular Basket

Before I begin to discuss the details of this handsome yet informal arrangement, I'd like to point out just what a difference good lighting can make to dried flower arrangements in general. The winter sunlight slanting through a low window in this photograph (see page 52) just catches the flowers with a ray of warmth and brings them memorably to life. The shadows in the background, too, add depth and charm to the arrangement. Always try to make sure that arrangements based on dried materials are well-

A Basket of Australian Wild Flowers

lit in one way or another: their muted colours need plenty of light. If you have dark corners that you want to fill then it's best to look for inspiration in the next chapter of the book, as dark conditions are where artificial flowers are most helpful.

I have chosen a wicker rectangular basket for this arrangement for a hallway or large sideboard. Bas-

kets are very popular containers for dried flower arrangements, and rightly so: somehow the colour and texture of the wicker and cane that baskets are so often made from partner dried flowers perfectly. But many baskets have rounded sides, and of course these need careful weighting and balancing to stop them toppling over. A basket of square dimensions like this may not be so useful for shopping, but it is perfect for flower arranging!

The first step is to wire a half brick of oasis sec into the middle of the basket. No lining is necessary, but remember to place a little sellotape over the block edge to stop the wire cutting into it after a time. Once this is secured, the dried materials can be inserted.

All of the materials have been air-dried with the exception of one pressed item: the three compound leaves from the paeonia suffruticosa (tree peony). As you'll see in the photograph, I've used a wide range of flowers of different shapes and sizes to maintain interest throughout the basket.

The basic principle in this arrangement is to position the stems so that they flow out from the handle arc; it is this feature of the basket that gives the arrangement its centre of gravity. The tallest point is set first with the delphinium (larkspur), and then the widest points follow using filipendula ulmaria (meadowsweet) and spiraea douglasii. Allow plenty of variation of length with these and all the other materials so that the flowers show to good advantage.

The five hydrangea heads were fitted into the arrangement early because they are difficult to thread in through the other stems. As a general principle, always remember to get difficult, stumpy or short-stemmed materials arranged first, leaving the thin stems and flower spikes to the last. "Difficult" in flower-arranging terms generally means wide and bulky flowers which do not thread easily into a small space; their petals, too, are liable to get torn and damaged. Large specimens of allium, heracleum

Dried Material in a Rectangular Basket

A Sand and Seashore Display

The seashore is an excellent place to find decorative materials, but I think I should point out that a number of the plants and stems we've used have never been near the seashore during their entire growing lives! They were simply things that seemed to me to be suitable for inclusion in this unusual collection.

AN ALTERNATIVE APPROACH TO ARRANGING

This is not, of course, an arrangement that everyone will want to have in their home: I don't think I'd particularly want it in mine! But it does illustrate some exciting possibilities, both for arrangements based on themes (such as the sea), and for the use of non-floral or non-plant material in arrangements. Even if you don't particularly want to reproduce this arrangement, you might consider doing something similar based around a theme of your choice. The only constraint is your imagination.

If you look carefully at the picture you will see that only a little real plant material has been used, most of the colour and interest coming from the other items: the shells in different shapes and colours, the pieces of coral, the starfish. All of these can easily be purchased from florists' sundriesmen, and in some cases bought or collected when away on holiday. (Shells are being used decoratively more and more today and I have recently seen some excellent flower pictures made entirely from shells of different sizes.)

To make this decoration, I have used as a base a large, interestingly shaped and knotted off-cut of wood: it is old and well-weathered with attractive contours of grain throughout. To hold the plant material, I have positioned a shallow pottery dish on this. Ideally, something quite heavy should be used so that it does not overbalance. Anything flat and strong will do because the dish will not show in the finished arrangement. In the base of the dish I have positioned a lump of Dri-hard, but one could also use potters' clay or a lump of oasis sec, provided it was carefully impaled on the special pinholder for oasis known as a "frog". (Do not ever try using an ordinary pinholder with oasis because it is useless.) Once the container is in the position you require, pour some dry silver sand around it to create the background. You will require quite a lot: over a bucketful. (It need not be wasted. Later on you may use it in your potting soil or for rooting cuttings.)

The first of the materials to fix in position are the two large flat fans of coral: this lace-like plant can be ordered in packets from a sundriesman. It is fragile but has a firm base which one can push well into the still-soft clay. These corals are available in both natural and dyed colours: use the natural colours for best results, as the artificial ones tend to look unreal. These coral fans begin the process of setting the outlines of the arrangement, and the three musa (banana) sticks are now positioned to complete the outline. These are the remains of the flower stem of the banana tree: they have been air-dried and sun-bleached, and have rugged whorl-like indentations.

FILLING OUT THE DISPLAY

The next materials I positioned were the free-floating stems of eryngium (sea holly): these, in fact, were grown in my own garden and air-dried. The other plant that I have used to fill the centre of the arrangement is known as feather smoke (I have been unable to find its correct botanical name). This rather fluffy material is ideal for filling in: it is soft and flowing and gives the impression of waving seaweed fronds. Behind the large shell on the right-hand side some genuine seaweed can be seen. This was air-dried. (A word of caution here: it was extremely pungent, even after having been washed in fresh water and dried out.) The shells I have used in the display are a personal choice: group them to make interesting patches of colour within the overall picture. The starfish to the left of the group, and the coral towards the centre, are also decorative

If you wished to increase the scale and scope of a decoration like this, you might like to try to fit in something like a fishing net to act as a background drape. There is no end to what can be done with imagination and a few dried flowers today. One point I would emphasize, though, is that it's important not to overdo the accessories. This is a failing of many people working in this area and depicting themes. There is always such a wealth of material that one could bring into a display that it's very important to know when to stop. It would be going too far, for example, to try to include a rowing boat here!

A Sand and Seashore Display

A Collection of Exotic Seedheads

Before I describe the details of this arrangement I have to confess that this is not a collection dear to me. At heart, I am a traditionalist: antiques, a country atmosphere and a comfortable home setting are what I chiefly treasure, and the very modern environment that an arrangement like this requires is not one I think I could be at ease in. That said, no one can deny that the materials used here are fascinating and compelling, in abstract terms, and if your tastes run to the unusual and the exotic then the creative possibilities offered by items like these are numerous.

The majority of this material came from a commercially available pack of assorted seedheads. It seemed to me, in both colouring and shape, that they would be best partnered by an intriguingly weathered piece of wood. Pieces of wood such as this are very useful: I am always looking out for them when walking in the country or by the sea. In this case I have used the remains of a tree trunk or old root system. It should be cleaned well with a stiff brush, and dried thoroughly before use so that it won't mark anything. You may find that it is easiest to fit it to a flat board which you have covered or coloured in some way. In this instance, the wood has been rested on dry, boat-shaped cocos (coconut) palm leaves on the left, and a dried lotus leaf on the right. The stems of these two dried leaves have been set in a block of Dri-hard. Oasis could have been used but a heavier medium like Dri-hard or clay will help prevent the arrangement from overbalancing.

The ornate staghorn-like materials that set the height of the arrangement are made from natraj, or fasciated bleached willow. The lotus seed pods at the centre of the arrangement are old favourites, and come in varying sizes. To the bottom right are a collection of ram's horn seed capsules (this is, I understand, a male palm which is split before drying). The pods that look rather like large pale lychees in the bottom left are from the aytocarpus heterophyllus (jack fruit) tree, while the centre upright stems with seed capsules at the top are banksia menzii cones. All these pods have, I believe, dried naturally in the warm climates in which they grow.

In all truth, not much arranging is required here. The taller materials, as mentioned earlier, are positioned after the width has been set by the dried leaves. The usual guideline of grouping similar materials together has been suspended as so few stems are involved; instead, aim for pleasing variety in height and shape. The grouping principle has been followed, though, in the case of the squatter seedheads and pods in the base of the arrangement; if the shapes are mingled, they would tend to fight with each other. Try to use the natural contours of the wood to harmonize with the contours of the materials. And, as always, don't overfill: the wooden base of the arrangement is an extremely attractive feature and it would be a shame to smother it with the eyecatching seedpods.

MATCHING THE BACKGROUND
The striking background to the arrangement is provided by two sorts of Japanese paper. Beneath the arrangement is a paper that includes trapped fibres, and behind the arrangement is a paper that includes fine wood shavings. Both partner the arrangement well, I feel.

A big advantage of this sort of arrangement, of course, is that it will certainly be long-lasting. Indeed I can see no reason why it shouldn't last forever! It would be easy to keep clean – regular dusting and an occasional wash would be all that was required.

Decorative Uses for Heracleum

Heracleum (known as hogweed or cow parsley) and in particular heracleum mantegazzianum (giant hogweed) has several eyecatching applications in dried flower terms. It dries naturally on the plant, but to retain its seedhead it should be cut when fully mature and air-dried carefully. (Handle with care: it can cause skin irritation.) The stems used for the large arrangement on page 69 were stood in a bicycle shelter to dry: moving air and protection from rain could be assured there. The seedhead could be sprayed with heavy duty lacquer or fine aerosol glue to hold the seed pods in position, but if you want a light effect to the decoration, allow the seeds to drop – you'll still be left with attractive stem clusters to the

A Collection of Exotic Seedheads

flower heads. One important point to remember is that the large hollow stems of heracleum are almost always home to several families of insects, so before bringing inside, spray well with a pesticide.

ARRANGING STEMS OF HERACLEUM

These stems have an architectural beauty all of their own, and they want to be displayed simply against a plain light background to be most effective. Originally, all the stems you see arranged were joined to just one large stem. This proved too large for the room in which they were to be sited, so I had to saw through this main stem and use the three side branches to add interest to the base of the group. The whole group was set up on a piece of plastic sheet to stop any marking of the polished wooden floor surface.

In the centre of this plastic sheet, an old tin tray was positioned, bearing a large lump of clay (or Dri-hard). The stems are carefully positioned in this. The main stem was the first to be set in place, at a pleasing

Seedheads in a Heracleum Vase (left)

An Arrangement of Heracleum Stems (right)

angle but without rendering the structure unsteady in any way. Stand back and look at the stem from all angles, then set in the extra side stems to balance and fill any awkward gaps. Now choose four or five large pieces of interesting rock: limestone is ideal for this. These rocks will help steady everything and support the weight of the main stem (though in actual fact it's not heavy and, once balanced, should stand up with

no difficulties). Set some clean, dry gravel amongst the stones, hiding any trace of the plastic sheet underneath. You could, if you wanted, add some silk foliage such as ferns, but I think that, as in most cases, the simplest finish is the best. (If you have dark walls, the heracleum could be plainly whitewashed, or painted before being glittered for a festive look.)

SETTING SEEDHEADS IN A HERACLEUM VASE
As assiduous readers of this chapter will already be aware, I am always looking out for new ideas for vases, bearing in mind that for dried flower arranging no vase need be watertight. It occurred to me, when cutting down the heracleum stems to fit the room setting as described above, that the lengths of hollow stem that remained might make original containers. Having dried them, I cut them into different lengths and attached them to a cork mat as a base. They glued together easily. To ensure stability, half-fill each stem with dry sand. As the photograph shows, I cut the tops of each heracleum section at an angle to allow more flow to the stems of the materials positioned inside, and also to reveal the different colour of the inside of the heracleum, which contributes to the overall effect. For extra strength, glue the sides of the cylinders as well as the bottoms.

Begin by inserting materials in the tallest tube and work down to the shortest one, making sure that plenty of interest goes into each. Vary height and shape, but do not overcrowd. There isn't really the potential for a true arrangement here, but a careful selection of stems going in the right direction will help to make a rustically pleasing group.

Pressed Flower Pictures

The two beautiful pictures seen on pages 70 and 71, made from pressed flowers, are the work of Joanna Sheen. Joanna was a student of mine some years ago, and now runs a company in South-West England producing a range of pictures like these for sale in England and abroad. I hasten to add that this is not

something we teach at the Constance Spry School, but I was delighted to find that Joanna's talents for flower arranging had blossomed, so to speak, in this way. Readers able to visit Chelsea Flower Show in London will be able to see Joanna's work there, and a list of retail stockists of her work is available by post.

I much appreciate her willing loan of these two lovely examples of her work for us to photograph and include in the book. The creation of pictures and designs made from pressed flowers and leaves is, of course, an important (if specialized) aspect of dried flower decoration, yet I was at first uncertain about including it in the book as I know I could not have produced anything of this quality myself. A great deal of talent and experience is needed for work at this level. Yet with care and patience, anyone should be able to produce a simple and attractive pressed flower picture. Here are some tips.

PRESSING FRESH FLOWERS AND LEAVES

The first thing to do, logically enough, is to press the flowers and foliage you'll need for your picture (though think carefully about the sort of materials you want – see my concluding remarks below). Be warned: pressing can be a slow and tedious business, in particular setting up the pieces carefully so that no room is wasted on each layer of the press. The materials should always be picked during the middle of the day when they are as dry as possible, and no rain should have fallen during the previous twenty-four hours. Grade the flowers for size and thickness and use only open single flowers. The petals of the flowers, and sprays of leaves, have to be correctly laid out on the paper: once pressed, you cannot change

their shape or disposition. Pressing time is anything from six to eight weeks. A certain amount of trial and error will be necessary with both timing and choice of flower varieties before really good results will be obtained. For example, I understand that delphinium (larkspur) flowers press well, while nigella (love-in-the-mist) tends to fade somewhat.

A SPOT OF GLUE

The glue that you use to affix the flowers is perhaps the most important item of all. It must hold the specimens well, yet be completely invisible when dry. A spot must be adequate to do the job. Pressed flower pictures have, of course, been made for many years and it appears that the beaten egg whites used in the past are still a very good fixing agent, but are not easy to use. Two proprietary brands that I have had some success with are Copydex and Reeves Greyhound PVA medium adhesive – but do remember to use only a very tiny amount. Always experiment first with your less successful pressed flowers, before risking all with your prize examples.

COLOURINGS AND VARIETIES

Two different frames have been chosen to suit the colour range of each group of flowers and leaves. The dark wood in the smaller photograph has a single rose species as the main flower, with wild rose leaves and little pieces of alchemilla. The oval gilt frame seen in the larger photograph to the right encloses a collection of single delphinium (larkspur) flowers, sprays of myosotis (forget-me-not) and potentilla anserina (silverweed).

There are a number of different ways of approaching the problem of framing your pressed flower work, just as there are of finding containers to position dried flowers in. My own way of proceeding would be first to choose the shape of the frame, then the colour or finish of the wood to suit the room in which it is to hang. Next decide on the style of arrangement you'd like, and finally select the actual materials you need to create the picture. In this way, you can control all of the important and expensive aspects of making your flower picture from the outset, and you will be able to wait until you have the materials you need before committing them to glass.

Pressed Flower Picture by Joanna Sheen

Pressed Flower Picture by Joanna Sheen

CHAPTER TWO

ARTIFICIAL FLOWER ARRANGEMENTS

Since Constance Spry herself first started making artificial flowers and plants back in the 1940s, the materials available to the flower arranger have undergone quite a revolution. As you will see from some of the arrangements at the end of this chapter, the original handmade waxed-paper flowers were works of art in their own right, with a price tag to match, but at least there is now an acceptable and affordable alternative in the latest generation of polyester silk flowers.

Tremendous progress has been made in terms of quality in the polyester silk field, and I think the German flowers, like those that have been used throughout this chapter for the photographed arrangements, are the best available. (My supplier is H. Andreas of Wiesentheid in West Germany: for the U.K. address, see page 4.) The colour range is surprisingly good and many can be taken for the real thing if used carefully. I remember using some in a mixed green plant collection in a dark corner at home where I have, quite frankly, always been unsuccessful with living material. They gave rise to considerable interest and even some requests for cuttings!

As I explained in the Introduction, it is possible to wash polyester silk flowers, but there are certain types on the market which contain a proportion of unwashable materials. The petals themselves, for example, may be of polyester silk, while foliage, sepals or stamens are made from a material that can't be moistened without losing colour or disintegrating. If you are in any doubt it is a good idea to try dampening a small area of each part of one of the plants to test it for colour fastness before immersing an entire collection in water.

Flowers for a Niche

A niche is an ideal setting for displaying an arrangement and is well worth considering when planning a room or hall design. Flowers placed in a niche are out of the way yet displayed at their best advantage. They can be illuminated from above if the niche is deep enough, to give the arrangement extra impact, and because niches always demand true "facing arrangements" you will only need the minimum number of flowers to make a lovely effect.

The container used here is one of my favourites, a cherub vase which seems to suit almost anything, from floral arrangements like this to simple mixed foliage. Displayed in a special setting like a niche, the container obviously plays an important part in the overall impression. It is still possible to find antique vases in this pattern from time to time, but the one shown here is a modern version. The small group of polyester flowers in the arrangement are set into a small piece of oasis sec with a layer of wire netting over the top, held in position with oasis tape.

Where the setting is as crucial as it is here, you should always work with the vase in position. Start by setting the height and the width, using two or three pieces of material at each point (botanically generalized white blossom has been used here), each stem being of slightly different length. Now begin to fill in the centre, using variegated peperomia, rose leaves and some stems of orange lily. Continue to fill the arrangement by working gradually down from the top, bringing the colours through the arrangement

Flowers for a Niche

from side to side. The varieties used here are convallaria (lily of the valley), convolvulus, champagne roses, pale yellow bellis perennis (daisies) and three pieces of dianthus (carnation) spray.

Even though this arrangement will not be viewed from the side, you should still remember to keep the floral fullness to the front of the vase, as illustrated on page 32. Think of the arrangement as an imaginary equilateral triangle, with the width from the central stems to the outside edges just under half the height of the tallest flower. All the stems should radiate from the centre and you should work some interesting curved pieces over the sides and front of the vase, hiding the hard outline of the rim.

A Table Centre in Silk

This unusual view of a table centre arrangement has been provided to give readers a very clear idea of one of the abiding principles of any flower arrangement, whether it uses fresh, dried or silk materials: the principle of the sweeping group. Each variety should be grouped and patterned so that the subjects recur or sweep through the arrangement from one side to the other. I should stress that this is not a cast-iron rule of flower arranging – Constance Spry herself did not like such rigidity – but rather a guideline to help you plan your progress through a design. The description given below of how this centrepiece was constructed should

A Table Centre in Silk

be regarded as guidance on how to approach a similar design of your own, rather than comprehensive instructions. It is unlikely that you will have exactly the same materials in any case, and you should always follow your own feelings when it comes to varying the content or design of any arrangement. With a few broad principles you will generally achieve much better results than you would by following a rigid pattern to the letter.

The container (which is, of course, invisible from this angle) is a shallow, oblong china trough, about 10 inches (25 centimetres) long, with rounded ends and a shell motif on the sides. As the materials are all in polyester silk and thus have wire stems, they are held in oasis sec. The piece of oasis sec is about 6 × 3 × 3 inches (15 × 7.5 × 7.5 centimetres); it is held in place with a layer of 2-inch (5-centimetre) wire netting over the top, and a little more around the edge of the container. The netting itself is secured in four places with either oasis tape or thin wire. The arrangement has been kept low, to make it ideal for a table setting, and you can judge its overall size by comparing it with the standard 10-inch (25-centimetre) dinner plate also in the picture.

MATCHING THE SETTING

The materials used in the arrangement are all items which are readily available in florists' or department stores, and they have been carefully chosen to blend with the colour scheme of their environment. You should always try to choose varieties that will work well with the colour scheme of the room in which the arrangement will appear. In this case it is also a good idea to make sure they tone in with the china and the table setting.

It is best to start with the foliage, so that you can get the large leaves well down in the arrangement from the beginning and then thread the flower stems in through them. (To help you understand how this table centre was put together, I have used the points of the compass to identify each part of the arrangement, taking the top of the picture as north, and so on.) The main foliage was placed at the widest points, with variegated hedera (ivy) running right across the centre from east to west and dryopteris (ladder fern) running from north-east to south-west. Rose leaves were run across from north-west to south-east, but you must be careful not to place them in blocks or they will give an unnatural, "set" look to the

arrangement. Finally, acer (maple) leaves were tucked deep down in the centre to hide any stems and oasis that were still showing.

The first flower stems to go in were the botanically generalized white blossom, running from east to west. Then the freesia was positioned, running from north-west to south-east. Being the most important flowers in the arrangement, the roses were kept largely in the centre with a few extra stems running from north to south. Single chrysanthemums were run across mainly from north-east to south-west and spray carnations from north-east to south-west.

This geographical description has been exaggerated to emphasize the point that subjects should sweep across the arrangement from side to side. In practice, the effect is much softer than this suggests and every leaf, stem and blossom should be encouraged to mingle into the overall scheme, with no one variety predominating.

THE MATERIALS YOU NEED

Just to give you an idea of the amount of material required for an arrangement like this, I used the following items for this table centre: nine roses with three additional buds; five sprays of freesia, with one flower and one stem of buds on each; three stems of small chrysanthemums with three to four flower heads on each; three bunches of spray carnations; three sprays of white blossom; three sprays of ivy; seven fronds of ladder fern; two sprays of rose leaves and one large trail of maple leaves. Choose top-quality examples: they will not be cheap, but they will look good and last a long time.

Sprays will naturally vary in size from one supplier to another, but you can always use any leftovers another time. Resist the temptation to use everything you have and thus overcrowd the arrangement. Provided you have been careful to hide the base of the stems, which are always unnatural features, every variety should show well.

Remember to shape up the stems before use, in order to get some movement into them. When you are cutting them into lengths try to cut back to a leaf joint or a bend. Always use wire cutters, which will help you to avoid leaving long, unsightly ends of plain wire. Everything should be treated as you would its fresh equivalent – the angle and movement of each stem should make it look as if it is in water and flowing from the centre of the arrangement.

Still Life with Flowers in an Urn

Titles like this are commonplace in many exhibition or art gallery catalogues. We are fortunate to have been left a rich heritage of these still-life paintings, a perfect blend of art and nature. Leafing through *The Glory of the Garden*, a beautifully illustrated catalogue brought out by the Royal Horticultural Society to accompany its exhibition of the same name, I have found plenty of inspiration. These magnificent paintings, the work of some of the most famous Dutch flower painters, like Jan van Huysum, Jan van Os, Rachel Ruysch, Jan Davidszoon de Heem and Gaspar Pieter Verbruggen, contain a wealth of detail in both shape and colour.

In some ways, they are often more of a botanical collection than a true flower arrangement, but even so a great deal of planning has gone into them. Seasons, of course, have been ignored, as they were painted over a long period, so they make ideal inspiration for artificial flower arrangements, where availability at different times of the year is not a problem. To achieve their flowing lines, soft effects and wonderful colour combinations (to say nothing of the insects, butterflies and birds' nests so often perfectly incorporated into the composition) they must have been very carefully sketched out in advance. With details like the bloom that brings the skin texture of any fruit in the paintings to life, and the soft, muddled centres of full-blown roses, peonies and hollyhocks, it is little wonder that so many of these wonderful works of art have been prized and preserved for centuries.

SOFT LIGHTING FOR A SUBTLE EFFECT

When I was lucky enough to receive a large group of German polyester silk flowers and foliage to work with, it inevitably brought these paintings to mind and I decided to try to make a still life "in the Flemish manner". I always enjoy using these materials because they are so realistic. Some are almost too good to be true and this lifelike colouring, paradoxically, can be a difficulty. Some of the paintings I have tried to imitate are over 300 years old, and beside the mellow, muted tones of these paintings many of the stems I have are a little too bright. With subtle lighting, however, and a suitable setting, they can be most effective.

The container I used was an old metal tulip-shaped urn on a square base. It is important to choose something appropriate but unobtrusive like this and reference to a book of colour prints of the original paintings will give you lots of ideas. Although the urn had a small metal lining, I discarded it so as to get the base of the arrangement further down into the container and so improve its stability. A block of oasis sec was placed on end, to help provide extra height to the stems at the back, with teased out moss pushed in around the sides. A layer of wire netting was fixed over the top to hold everything firm.

POSITIONING THE MAIN MATERIALS

The placing of individual flowers in an arrangement like this is really controlled by the length of the stems. You can, of course, attach pieces to false stems but in this instance I did not think it necessary. The height was set with a stem of white lilium speciosum (lily) in the centre, with a stem of blue agapanthus (African lily) to the right and an iris germanica (purple flag) to the left. A stem of white antirrhinum (snapdragon) was placed directly in front of the lily. As the container is rather narrow and the planned group rather large, these first stems had to be placed right at the back to make room for everything else. At the top right I inserted a stem of prunus blossom (ornamental cherry), while a stem of blue campanula (bellflower) established the widest point on the right. On the left this was echoed with another stem of ornamental cherry and some more lily. To fill the centre and create a background for the rest of the arrangement I used a codiaeum plant (croton). If you study the original still-life paintings closely you will find that very little foliage was included. With artificial flowers, however, something is needed to hide the unsightly wire stems at the base and to avoid a "bare" look at the centre of the arrangement, and croton fitted the bill for this. Next I added the pale-pink peony deep in the centre and the fuchsia coming right over the front of the vase. The blue clematis on the bottom left and the white phalaenopsis on the bottom right were the final touches in setting the outlines of this large arrangement.

Still Life with Flowers in an Urn

FILLING IN THE DETAIL

Now it was time to fill in the detail, introducing as much interest as possible with a wide variety of colours and shapes. On the left this included a single vermilion papaver nudicaule (Iceland poppy), a stem of yellow freesia, a head of hydrangea, some peachy-coloured alstroemeria (Peruvian lily) and a few zinnia flowers. An apricot gerbera and another pink peony in front of the ornamental cherry blossom at the top right was followed by yellow iris xiphium (Spanish iris), another stem of yellow freesia and a large white iris pallida (bearded iris). At the bottom right I put in another hydrangea head and some stems of pale pink apple blossom. The centre is dominated by the exotic anthurium, with its striking, heart-shaped spathe, the blue iris xiphium and a stem of spotted white lilium auratum (golden-rayed lily).

Like the group described on page 72 this is a facing arrangement and is ideal for a large niche or alcove. In fact, it *must* be seen from the front because of the way the stems have been set in the vase. From the side it would look very odd.

A Victorian Glass Dome

Glass domes like the one pictured opposite were a popular feature in many Victorian households. Often used, I'm sorry to say, to display stuffed birds, they came in a variety of shapes and sizes. A large bird or a collection of two or three smaller ones were placed in the larger round or oval domes amongst a realistic setting of foliage and dried grasses or perhaps perched on a suitable branch. Often the back of the dome was painted to give an impression of the appropriate habitat. Another use was found for smaller, shallow, round domes as long-lasting decorations for a grave, containing a posy of white fabric or unglazed china flowers. Today, domes are back in fashion, thankfully in the less morbid role of housing dried or artificial flowers for home decoration.

ANTIQUE DOMES

I own a small dome containing some Constance Spry handmade flowers. This piece (not illustrated here) was made, well over twenty years ago, by a special department of the organization. Different flowers, fruits and foliages were made individually from waxed paper, and they were then joined together to make a cone of plants. This is a gift I will always treasure and you will see why if you look at the photograph of it which appears on page 139 of *The Constance Spry Book of Flower Arranging* (Sundial Publications, 1979, and Octopus Books, 1985).

Antique domes on well-turned wooden bases are not easy to find these days, but you can get hold of thicker glass or perspex domes from some suppliers of dried and artificial flowers. The dome I have used here is, in fact, an authentic Victorian one. Its thin, fine glass and elegant proportions are the chief clues to its authenticity and I have added the finishing touches with a black velvet ribbon around the rim of the glass and a black plaited cord around the edge of the lovely ebony base.

MAKING THE MOST OF CONSTRAINTS

Like the still-life arrangement on page 77 this is in some ways more of a collection than an arrangement, because all the material must be fitted neatly into the confined space rather than arranged within it. The group has been set up in an antique night-light stand, which consists of a small glass dish in a gilded metal stand, fixed to a round, bevelled mirror base. This is another favourite from Constance Spry's collection of vases at Winkfield. Whatever you decide to use, be careful to choose a suitable container. A small milk glass or a pretty basket-shaped vase, for example, would both look right, but rough pottery or basket-ware would definitely be out of place. Delicate, elegant lines are required, so china, glass or metal are probably the right materials to look for.

The stems are all fixed into a round of oasis. I have chosen a mixture of polyester silks and dried materials for this soft, green, white and cream decoration. To make the arrangement, I stood the container next to the glass dome to help judge the dimensions correctly. As you go along, it is important to check the size from time to time by slipping the dome over the unfinished group. The arrangement can be made as a facing or, better still, an all-round group but it must be given a severe cone shape to match the space within the dome. Being a decidedly upright arrangement, you will need quite a few tall stems like the various grasses I have used here.

A Victorian Glass Dome

First of all, I set the height with some stems of white delphinium consolida (larkspur), being careful to allow for the curve at the top of the dome. Next I put in the polyester silk begonia rex leaves and white roses, working with them at different lengths but being sure to get some of them tucked deep down into the centre of the arrangement to add visual weight. Then the other flowers – white achillea (yarrow) and helichrysum – were added around the sides, together with some muscari (grape hyacinth) seedheads. When positioning the flowers, remember that they should not touch the sides of the glass in the finished arrangement, so keep stopping to cover everything with the glass dome before proceeding any further. In general, this material can be placed as you would in any flower group but it must be kept tucked in more tightly than usual. Finally, I added the thin stems of briza media (quaking grass) and lagurus ovatus (hare's tail grass), which can be easily pushed in between the other items.

FITTING OVER THE DOME

When you have finished the arrangement, it is a good idea to find someone to help with the dome itself. Ask them to lower the glass down slowly while you push any wayward stems carefully into place. Once under the glass, the decoration will last for years. No dust or insects can get in to mark or damage the contents in any way and, provided you have been working with absolutely dry material in the dry atmosphere that is usually found in modern centrally-heated homes, condensation will not be a problem. The only maintenance required is to dust the dome from time to time to keep the glass bright and clean.

Artificial Houseplants in a Terracotta Trough

There has been a great revival of interest in pots and troughs recently, with a wide variety of new patterns and designs coming on to the market. Terracotta, the material from which the trough seen on page 81 has been made, is attractive but there are many alternatives and it is always worth looking round for something that suits the colours of the setting in which you plan to use it. Containers should be chosen with just as much care as the plants you are going to display in them when considering colour schemes and textures. Every element is important in determining the overall effect of a floral decoration.

When buying a trough or container like this it is always wise to plan for real plants, whose demands are naturally more complex than their artificial counterparts. Even if you intend initially to use polyester silk plants, you may well decide to change them for living plants eventually and then it will be important to have proper drainage holes, for example.

PERFECT FOR A PATIO

The group shown here could be an ideal display for the patio, if well protected, or could be placed in a sun room or conservatory where it would receive plenty of good light and would stay quite warm. The codiaeum (croton) is the most difficult subject, requiring a fairly humid atmosphere and a temperature of 13°C (55°F), and being susceptible to draughts and sudden changes in temperature. The nephrolepis (Boston fern) and the fuchsia would also appreciate moist conditions while the cyperus alternifolius (umbrella plant) thrives with plenty of moisture. A trough as deep as the one shown here will hold plenty of soil and consequently won't dry out too quickly. The other foliage plants – tradescantia, zebrina, hedera helix (ivy) and dieffenbachia (dumb cane) – are easy to cultivate under normal growing conditions. Cyclamen is not such a seasonal plant these days, with specimens available on and off throughout the year (usually to coincide with Easter, Mother's Day and other similar occasions) rather than just in the winter and early spring. If you were unable to find one at the right time, a begonia would do as an alternative. The trailing plants, like the ivy and the tradescantia, help to soften the outline and reduce the rather upright appearance of such a deep container.

From a description like that, coupled with the photograph opposite, it would be easy enough to believe that what we are looking at are living plants. In fact, they are examples of the excellent polyester silk plants that are now among the most important artificial materials in use for decorations. Some of the taller plants are made up on real (dried or woody) stems, while others are completely artificial. Many of them are very expensive, especially when used in large groups, but the initial outlay is soon offset by their durability and indifference to lighting and atmospheric conditions, and they have consequently become a popular feature of interior design in office buildings and business premises.

Before you start to make up a display like this you should decide where it will be placed and what shapes, colours, textures and growing habits would be suitable there. For a hot, sunny area cacti and other succulents might be appropriate, for example, while softer fern-like materials could suit a greener, cooler atmosphere. Some people enjoy foliage plants on their own, while others feel deprived without the splashes of colour provided by a flowering plant or two. The choice, of course, is yours, but you should always look for variety and interest whatever the range. Some plants come already fixed into a pot, while others simply have their stems bound into a plastic wrap. The former are not a problem, provided the pots are not too wide to drop into the trough. One or two ready-potted plants, in fact, help to fill the spaces and solve the perennial problem of anchoring loose stems.

PACKING AND POSITIONING

With a deep trough it is a good idea to start by placing a close-fitting piece of cardboard in the base followed by a layer of screwed-up newspaper, wood-wool (the fine pine-shavings often used for packing) or polystyrene packing shapes held in a plastic bag. Once you have planned the layout of plants in the trough to ensure you will get the best display from them, gradually start to work them into the packing material. If the arrangement is to have a "back" and a "front", place the tall items in first, towards the back. Here I used the croton and the umbrella plant to establish the height and then placed the tradescantia and zebrina at the sides, with the ivy trailing over the front. As each plant is put into place, turn and shape it to produce the best effect. Remember that stems and leaves can be bent and moved to bring them to life. This is where horticultural experience and a good eye for detail come into their own. If you find it difficult to produce a lifelike appearance go and examine the plant in a greenhouse or a nursery, or look at photographs in gardening books. Tradescantia and zebrina can be bought as a packet of five to ten single stems, which can be cut and shaped to make up a plant in much the same way as you would produce cuttings from the live plant!

COLOUR FOR THE CENTRE

In the centre of the group, from left to right, I have used a dumb cane, a cyclamen (the foliage of this plant is particularly good), a Boston fern planted at the back but with a few fronds pulled to the front, and a fuchsia. When all the plants are in place and you are

Artificial Houseplants in a Terracotta Trough

satisfied with the disposition of each leaf and stem, it is time to fill in all the spaces with artificial compost or stone granules. This is special light-weight material made from burnt cork and available through stockists of artificial plants. Firm the bedding down to hold the plants securely and dust off any pieces that have fallen on to the leaves. Stand back to assess your efforts from a little distance and then adjust the odd leaf here and there to obtain a lifelike, "growing" appearance.

With careful attention and green fingers it is possible, of course, to produce a long-lasting version using living plants. There can be difficulties, however, in providing the right growing conditions for a mixture of plants with varying requirements. This can be solved by isolating some of them in individual pots, but with artificial plants the problem never arises. Do watch out, though, for over-zealous friends trying to water them in your absence!

An All-Round Arrangement in a Shallow Dish

This attractive arrangement is ideal for a low coffee-table, a window-sill or a wide shelf. It could be made up with growing plants or, as shown here, with realistic artificial ones. Whatever you are using it is a good idea to include one or two flowering plants. If they are living they can be replaced when the flowers are finished to freshen up the arrangement, and if they are artificial they can be changed to alter the colour scheme. With this kind of attention you can make either type of arrangement last six months to a year before any major overhaul is necessary.

The container I have used for this group is a round, shallow ceramic dish, which I brought back from a visit to Japan. Much the same sort of thing can be purchased elsewhere, however, made by local pottery designers. If you are interested and have the opportunity to try making something similar yourself, a shallow dish is much easier to make than a pot which has to be thrown on a potter's wheel. Making your own container adds an extra, personal dimension to any arrangement you have created yourself.

A shallow basket lined with plastic or a painted metal or fibreglass tray would be an acceptable alternative and, although I prefer a round container for this arrangement, you could even use a rectangular plastic seed tray, which is very easily obtained from any garden centre. Whatever you use, do stand it on a cork mat or a piece of felt to avoid scratching polished or painted surfaces. You should also watch out for any signs of dampness on the container when in use because moisture can build up through condensation in certain conditions, which can also damage your furniture. In theory there is no ideal size for this type of decoration but it should not be too large or it will prove difficult to move for cleaning. An overall diameter of about 2 feet (60 centimetres) is about right, as in the arrangement shown here. For this size you will need about seven plants, plus an assortment of stones and bark to hold them in place. Stones and bark also add to the range of shapes and textures in the design.

Whether you are using live or artificial plants, the first step is to fill the base of the dish with some good potting compost and then position one or two large pieces of rock or stone. These should be chosen carefully for colour as well as shape. Limestone is the right sort of colour but you should avoid dark stone like granite which would be much too sombre. These will help to hold the arrangement together, so they should be pushed down into the compost to keep them firmly in place.

CREATING A PICTURE

Before starting to position the plants hold them up to get an idea of colour, shape and proportion. You are about to create a picture, just as you would with cut flowers in a vase, so you should plan the arrangement out carefully in advance. As artificial plants have no root-ball to anchor them in the potting medium, it is necessary to provide an alternative. A piece of soaked oasis can be used but you must remember to keep it damp. Position it in the compost to hold the plants firm. You can also use a piece of Dri-hard rolled into a ball: push the stem into it while it is still soft and it will soon set hard. In this case, of course, the soil can be kept dry but it is a good idea to set the Dri-hard on to a piece of cardboard, to prevent it damaging the container and to make it easy to lift the plant out later if you wish to replace it.

For this arrangement I placed a chlorophytum (spider plant) and a sansevieria (mother-in-law's tongue) at the back to provide some height, with a colourful aglaonema on the left at the front. The other foliage plants are a deep-green zebrina with purple-tinged variegation to the left and a tradescantia and nephrolepis (Boston fern) on the right. In the centre, as the floral focal point of the group, I used a vanda orchid. As the plants were placed in position I added a few more smaller pieces of stone and one or two pieces of cork bark. Gravel and sand add extra interest and lichen or bun moss are useful for hiding the soil. If you keep the lichen or moss damp they will add still more colour to the arrangement.

SHAPING INTO LIFE

Once the plants are all set into position your horticultural knowledge and artistic touch come into operation. Everything must be bent, curled and twisted into a really lifelike appearance. The stems must be shaped to look like growing plants and the low-growing trailing plants must tumble over the rim of the container. The orchid may need a cane to support the flower stem – and why not? You would have to use one if it were real.

An All-Round Arrangement in a Shallow Dish

After a time you may want to change one or two plants. Other plants that would be suitable for such an arrangement include different varieties of hedera (ivy), flowering begonia or begonia rex, fuchsia, spathiphyllum (peace lily), varieties of fern, peperomia, azalea, streptocarpus (Cape primrose) or cyclamen. In springtime you could replace the orchid with a group of bulbs.

If you decide to create something like this using fresh materials, it is a good idea to consider using a flowering pot plant as the floral centrepiece of the arrangement. Provided the compost is deep enough in the centre (it helps if you choose shallow-potted specimens) and there is enough surrounding foliage to hide the rim, the pot itself (with the plant in it) can simply be pushed down into place. Once the blooms have died away, you can simply lift out the pot and replace it with another pot plant.

Japanese Tree Peony and Lilies in an Alabaster Vase

This group, which I arranged in this vase well over twenty years ago, is one of my greatest favourites. The elements were a collection of leftover oddments from a display organized by the Constance Spry Handmade Flower Department at a London exhibition. In spite of such apparently unpromising origins, however, I could see straight away that they would make up a "picture" once I had assembled them in a suitable arrangement – quite a large one, as it turned out, measuring approximately 3 feet (90 centimetres) high by 2 feet 6 inches (75 centimetres) wide.

Handmade flowers do lose their colour after a while and it can be difficult to keep cleaning them year after year without their wax surface becoming damaged. An additional problem with the white and pale-coloured papers used in making the petals is that they become discoloured with age. I am worried that it will prove difficult to repaint them, even though Monique Regester (see pages 88–93) assures me that repairs are possible. One day I will have to do something to restore them. They now have an antique look about them when closely examined, although it is difficult to spot any blemishes from the photograph opposite. In fact, I find their old, mellowed look attractive and would not part with them at any price – by now they are virtually irreplaceable.

SUITABLE SUBJECTS FOR PAPER AND WAX

If you study each of the components of this group it does appear that the subjects lend themselves very well to imitation in paper and wax. The shapes are fairly simple and even the natural living plants have a slightly waxy appearance. However well the hand-made plants are made, the materials and the process used makes it inevitable that naturally fine, thin leaves and petals will look, when modelled, gross and clumsy. Consequently, the best subjects for this type of treatment are those that have fleshier components and a smooth, glossy finish that will be echoed by the appearance of the wax. The painting is obviously very important in determining the realism of the finished product. In this group the variegation of the hosta leaf and the pink tinge on the edge of the bergenia are particularly well observed and executed. The effect with all of these plants is stunningly lifelike and I can still remember quite vividly the original display of peonies at the exhibition, grouped on their own in a

shallow dish and set against a Japanese wallpaper and a wonderful lacquered screen.

The container I used is a bowl-shaped vase made of unpolished alabaster, with a pedestal and a narrow neck, which I had brought from Jerusalem for me many years ago. It would be impossible to find any lining for it so it could never hold water (alabaster tends to crack and disintegrate if unlined and left in contact with water), but it is ideal for an arrangement of artificial flowers like this. The simple shape and rather crude finish of the unpolished stone blend in well with the "patina" that time has given the collection and they make an attractive display set on a small round table in my sitting room.

ARRANGING THE COMPONENTS

Assembling the group was quite simple. Into the container I placed a ball of 2-inch (5-centimetre) wire netting. The two stems of camellia foliage went in first, one at the top and one on the right-hand side, both leaning back slightly. Then I put in the two compound stems of hedera helix (ivy) on the left and the larger-flowered clematis on the right. Now the taller lilium longiflorum (Easter lily) went in at the back together with the large single leaves of hosta (plantain lily) and bergenia which form the centre of the group. Remember that when leaves and flowers are mounted on wire stems they can be adjusted slightly after they have been threaded into the netting, whereas fresh stems can snap when manipulated like this.

Next I set the bottom paeonia (peony) deep down in the centre of the arrangement, to hide the hard rim of the vase and to integrate plants and container into a unified whole. Finally, I positioned the second lily and the two other peonies together with the smaller-flowered clematis montana and the remaining stems of ivy, bringing one or two pieces well out over the front.

It gives me great pleasure to see these beautiful plants permanently recorded in this photograph. They are inevitably deteriorating as the years go by and I would hate to think that I might be deprived of these reminders of the wonderful times I had when the "Arts", as the artificial plant department was known in those days, shared the Constance Spry School building with me in London.

Japanese Tree Peony and Lilies in an Alabaster Vase

A Cherub Holding Fruit and Foliage

This is another arrangement which must be at least twenty years old. I actually made some of the material myself, under strict supervision, and I can assure you that it is much easier to arrange than to make! Handmade plants of any kind demand a great deal of exacting work to create the detail of specimens like these and the shaping, colouring and wax finishing is a highly skilled technique. Sadly, it is one which is dwindling rapidly as the demand for such high quality but expensive materials diminishes. Monique Regester (see pages 88–93) is one of the last commercial practitioners of this delicate art.

Just to give you an example of the intricacy of the work, I will describe how each of the redcurrants is made. The berry itself is formed from cotton wool, mounted on a fine stem. Each one is painted singly to get the range of colour and ripeness. If you examine a fresh redcurrant you will see that the remains of the flower calyx appears at the tip and for the handmade fruit this tiny structure must be cut out of paper, painted and then fixed to the berry with tweezers. Finally, the individual fruits are waxed and then mounted up into sprays. The blackberries, too, are made from cotton wool and then covered with seed capsules, applied and painted singly, to imitate the structure of the fresh fruit. Then the stems are wired together into sprays. As you can see from the picture opposite, some of the blackberry sprays include one or two open flowers too, in the search for an even closer mimicry of the natural prototype. The larger fruits are also made from cotton wool but to achieve the required shape they are wrapped in a crepe paper binding before being painted and waxed. Everything is modelled closely on the fresh original to ensure that the result is as realistic as possible.

THE ART OF OBSERVATION

If you examine the photograph closely, you will begin to understand the kind of skill involved in such accurate modelling. Many techniques are needed – painting, waxing, shaping and so on – but the most valuable ability of all is one which any good flower arranger should possess to some degree: an aptitude for careful observation. Apart from the luscious

ripeness of the grapes and plums in this arrangement, achieved with smooth surfaces and continuous curves, and the convincing realism of the blackberries, where the colouring of each berry on the spray shows a slightly different stage of maturity, even so simple a thing as the disposition of stems, leaves and fruit has been perfectly captured. Although the fruit, with its cotton wool centre, is actually as light as a feather, by bending the stems in just the right way the arrangement has been given the appearance of a group of autumn branches laden with a heavy harvest, the fruit hanging down as if inviting you to pick it.

DWINDLING DEMAND

At the time when the materials used in this arrangement were being made, the Constance Spry workshop sent fruit and flowers all over the world to act as props in advertising photographs. Today, fresh fruit of almost any kind is available throughout the year so there is much less demand for this sort of work. The time involved in making each of these handmade fruits, of course, makes them very expensive (a group like the one shown here would cost several hundred pounds nowadays), but the quality does show. As with the real thing, each fruit is slightly different from its neighbour, unlike the modern plastic varieties which are unnaturally identical. Even the attempts to grade fresh supplies that one sees so much these days cannot achieve such perfect regimentation.

The container I used for the arrangement was another Italian cherub vase, but a much larger one than that shown on page 73. The cherub is holding a shell, which I filled with teased-out sphagnum moss rolled in a ball of wire netting, which is then clad in more sphagnum moss. This was then wired firmly into place, making a much longer lasting support than oasis, which tends to disintegrate after a while.

Originally, I made the arrangement to stand on my mother's sideboard, so it was really only going to be viewed from the front. It is shown here on a small chest of drawers in my dining room, but if you are going to display something like this where it can be seen from the sides as well as from head-on you will need to add more material, facing round slightly towards the back, to give an all-round effect.

First of all, I established the height by setting in

A Cherub Holding Fruit and Foliage

the back stem of vine foliage followed by the sprays of apple on the top left and plum on the top right. Then I inserted the sprays of orange in the centre, together with a few individual vine leaves to create pockets for the loose fruits. The grapes and redcurrants were then worked in at the base, coming right down over the front of the vase. The back and sides were filled in from the top downwards: blackberries and red plums on the left and more orange and apple on the right. Finally, the individual fruits tucked into the centre included a pineapple, a pear and even a pomegranate. Some of the larger fruits have been mounted on a wire in the base which was simply pushed into the moss.

There are two problems with maintaining a beautiful decoration like this if it is not protected. The first, of course, is dust, as it is impossible to wash anything like the peaches or grapes without destroying their natural-looking bloom. The second I find more difficult to accept. This is that a surprisingly large number of people will rush up to the display and squeeze the fruit, exclaiming "Is it real?" If you are ever lucky enough to own a collection like this and wish to avoid the fruit being spoiled because the wax has been cracked, then a glass dome would be a wise investment. The alternative is a sign like that at my greengrocer's: "Don't squeeze me till I'm yours"!

Waxed Paper Magnolias

As proof that handmade wax flowers are still being made today, and as beautifully as ever, I am delighted to be able to include the next three arrangements in the book. They are all the work of Monique Regester, a member of the Constance Spry handmade flower department in its last days, and a commercial practitioner of this art ever since. Monique produces a wide range of work for both commercial and private clients, and her address is given on page 4.

I discovered her work again quite by chance during the early stages of this book's creation. Passing the window display of a well-known London jeweller I happened to notice a small arrangement of spring flowers. On close inspection I was certain that these artificial plants were the handiwork of someone with a Constance Spry training. The assistant in the shop was most helpful when I asked who had made them. When I contacted Monique she said she remembered me from her days in the 20-strong handmade flower department. It was their job to make up perfect imitations of flowers, foliage and fruit from paper and wax, and I am thrilled to be able to present these modern examples of that highly skilled technique through Monique's generous loan of three of her arrangements.

SIMPLE SHAPES AND PERFECT DETAILS
The magnolia stems are held in place by a small piece of oasis sec, covered in sphagnum moss and placed in a small, boat-shaped china vase. Each flower is so perfectly shaped and realistically detailed that it is difficult to believe they are artificial waxed paper imitations wired on to real stems. As I pointed out on page 84, certain plants lend themselves very well to this technique and magnolias, with their waxy cup-like flowers, definitely fall into this category. The bold, simple shapes of the petals, the fleshy pistil and wine-coloured stamens are perfect in every detail. The rosy flush at the base of each flower probably identifies them as magnolia × soulangiana, but it would need to be a very good spring indeed to get so many blooms of such good quality, without at least some showing signs of frost damage at the tips.

WAXING CRITICAL
Monique says that the waxing is, for her, the most critical part of the whole process, as it is at this stage that so many things can go wrong and many hours of work spent cutting, shaping and painting can go to waste. Many flowers – such as those in the spring collection shown on page 93 – need only one or two dips in wax; magnolias, on the other hand, need up to five wax coats to give a really lifelike sheen to the sumptuous, fleshy petals.

The elegant, flowing lines of the dark branches make a wonderful contrast to the flowers and the fresh young leaves just beginning to appear seem to be bursting out of the real stems on which they have been mounted. The vase could, perhaps, have been a little more substantial to prevent it being overpowered by such a striking display, but wherever you group specimens like these they should always be used alone. Their bold simplicity should be left to speak for itself.

Waxed Paper Magnolias by Monique Regester

THE FRESH ALTERNATIVE

Provided you are not over-fussy about perfect blooms throughout, this is another arrangement that could be produced from fresh materials. To achieve the stark contrast of open flowers against a tracery of almost bare branches you will need to use one of the deciduous varieties, such as magnolia salicifolia or magnolia × soulangiana, rather than the evergreen magnolia grandiflora. It is a good idea to plant these early-flowering trees in a reasonably sheltered spot to minimize frost damage to the unopened buds. They can also be grown as wall shrubs, providing even more protection. Try displaying them in a tall, cylindrical vase and remember to peel away the tough outer bark at the base of each stem to help ensure that sufficient water flows up to the blooms. An arrangement like this has a certain oriental feel to it – appropriately enough, as so many of the varieties originate from Japan – and looks particularly good in uncluttered, modern surroundings.

A Country Collection

Standing only 12 inches (30 centimetres) high, this charming group of handmade plants is the second example of Monique Regester's beautiful work. The quail eggs give a good idea of its size and of the amount of minute detail crammed into such a small arrangement. If you are very observant you may have spotted one deviation from the country theme. At the top left and the bottom right, Monique has included two flowers of cobaea scandens (cathedral bell), a vigorous climber from the flower garden and a favourite of Constance Spry.

It was one of Constance Spry's beliefs, however, that flower arranging is your opportunity to express what *you* believe to be beautiful, and in doing so you should be free from inhibition. If you think a particular plant would suit the group you are creating, then you should include it. No doubt Monique felt that these gorgeous pink and green bells would tone in perfectly with the colours and shapes of the other climbing plants, and I must admit I'm in full agreement with her: they certainly add interest to the group. Seen here it is easy to imagine this particular specimen as a wayward "garden escape", growing among its more rural neighbours at the edge of a cottage garden.

It is in the cobea that a number of Monique's exceptional talents can be seen clearly. The painting – done using thinned oil paints – is very fine and delicate, in particular the striations where the petal colour alters from green to purple. Monique paints the flowers and leaves as many as five times: first of all a colour wash, then several sessions for highlights, followed by another two for veining and edging. The painting is generally done directly onto the already-modelled flower – and the shaping of the cobea, I feel, is also noteworthy. The stamens, finally, are another triumph, with their midsummer loads of creamy yellow pollen. Note, too, the filigree stamens on the clematis vitalba (wild clematis).

AN UNUSUAL AND INTERESTING SUBJECT

Cobaea itself is an interesting plant for the flower arranger, whether fresh or artificial. The green, saucer-shaped calyx remains after the flower has dropped and is very decorative. It is usually grown as an annual, though it is really a half-hardy perennial. Protected under glass it can be grown as a perennial,

provided you can give it a lot of space, as the growth is vigorous and a mature plant can reach 20 feet (6 metres) or more in height. It supports itself in much the same way as sweet peas do with branched tendrils, and should be trained up netting or trelliswork. If you can provide a minimum winter temperature of at least 5°C (41°F) the plant will remain evergreen. In the open garden, choose a sunny, sheltered position and try to give protection from winter frosts and you may well be rewarded with a profuse harvest of blooms. It has a long flowering period but I was still astonished on one occasion to find a specimen in my garden in full flower on 1st January – more realistically, you could expect to see flowers from May through till October.

The container here is a little china urn and Monique has simply filled it with a ball of moss to hold the stems. The height and width of the group was established with stems of clematis vitalba, and hops and convolvulus have been used in sweeping lines across from bottom left to top right. The blackberry stems give support to the whole arrangement, with a couple of stems tucked deep down in the centre and coming out over the rim of the vase. This helps to establish the story behind the group, too – the very tip of a wild bramble hedge, perhaps, with climbers twining their way into the sunlight at the top. The cobaea adds interest and was probably pushed in last of all, to complete the arrangement.

MATERIAL IN THE SPRY TRADITION

All of these plants are well worth considering for fresh, as well as artificial groups. Hops, for example, are not very common as garden plants, yet they can be used fresh in the autumn or dried during the winter and their unusual flowers are an interesting addition to many arrangements. (The delicate modelling Monique has achieved in order to successfully mimic the interlocking petals of the top flowers is another impressive aspect of this collection.) The clematis is often used in later maturity, when the flowers have begun to turn "fluffy", but I prefer them in this simple, just-opened state. A suitable alternative to this wild species would be one of the smaller garden varieties, such as clematis flammula, with its pure white, scented flowers, and the more usual clematis montana. Fruit always adds interest to an arrangement of

A Country Collection by Monique Regester

flowers and these realistic handmade blackberries – again, note the various stages of maturity of the fruit – look very attractive. The time required to make artificial work at this level of technical expertise, of course, means that it is very expensive – but worth every penny.

The materials in this group are all very firmly in the Constance Spry tradition. Whenever I look into the box of relics from my early days at the School I find species like these very much in evidence, and I can still remember the sight of similar stems of con-volvulus trailing from baskets in Piccadilly's Burl-ington Arcade at the time of Queen Elizabeth's Coronation in 1952. The flowers, sadly, have long been gone but I think I still have one of the baskets around somewhere!

A Trough of Spring Flowers

A seasonal arrangement like this can be a wonderful way to conjure up your favourite time of year a little in advance. For some people this will be the spring – they can hardly wait to get through the cold, dark days of winter. Others crave for summer sunshine, while many love the rich and mellow autumn. Few can find many good words to say about winter, but even then there is much to be found for an attractive, seasonal group, as I hope the next chapter of this book will demonstrate. Constance Spry used to love the tracery of bare branches and the often unexpected delight of discovering the first aconites and snowdrops of the year braving the elements.

This group of spring flowers is the third and last example of Monique Regester's exquisite handwork that we have been lucky enough to be able to include in this book. The container is a bonsai trough and into this has been set a bed of sphagnum moss. The bark completes the framework, adding both height and interest. Grouped around the bark are the taller subjects, the daffodils and the narcissus, while snowdrops, primroses and cyclamen have been placed along the front of the trough. Ivy has been used to soften the edges of the group, trailing over the front of the trough and lessening the otherwise rather upright feeling of these brave new spring flowers.

IMITATING GROWING PLANTS

A bed of sphagnum moss, or even potting compost covered with a thin layer of moss, is always a good choice for an arrangement of artificial materials like this if you wish to simulate growing plants. One of the most difficult areas in which to achieve a lifelike effect is the point where the plant meets the soil. Ideally, it should appear to be springing out of the ground, but so often it is difficult to avoid the startled look of a stem simply pushed into a supporting medium. The moss successfully hides the join, particularly if you ease the plant down, turning it as you do so, until the point where you would expect to find the leaves and stems of a real plant growing out of the ground is just beneath the surface.

Once more the craftsmanship shown in these plants is astonishing. If you compare them with the polyester silk materials used in the spring arrangement on page 113 the quality and detail immediately become apparent. The marbling of the cyclamen leaves is another beautiful touch, adding to the delicacy of the group. An important part of the realism, of course, lies in the disposition of the leaves, stems and flowers. The cyclamen, for example, with their graceful swan necks and pretty, turned back petals, are almost an arrangement in themselves. The snowdrops, too, capture perfectly the graceful, drooping heads of the natural prototype, while the daffodils turn their faces unashamedly towards the spring sunshine. A detail I'm particularly fond of is that of the papery bud husk of these tiny early daffodils curling off behind the flower: beautifully observed by Monique and achieved by some mysterious means that only she would know, I'm sure. Again, three quail eggs indicate the tiny scale – the entire arrangement is barely 6 inches (15 centimetres) high.

ALTERNATIVE APPROACHES

Another approach you could try for a seasonal arrangement like this – and such an arrangement could easily be made using polyester silk materials rather than waxed paper flowers – would be to create a little spring "garden" in a shallow round dish, or even an oval meat plate. First the height could be established with a branch of hazel catkins or pussy willow fixed into a piece of Plasticine or Dri-hard. Then a bed of damp bun moss would be placed in the dish with gravel, bark and small stones for variety of colour, shape and texture. Plants you could tuck down into this setting would include aconitum (monkshood), crocus, primula vulgaris (primrose), scilla, tulipa clusiana (lady tulip) and hyacinthus orientalis albulus (Roman hyacinth). Foliage would include various forms of hedera (ivy) and tradescantia. With plenty of material and room to display it this could make the perfect arrangement for a low coffee table or even a dining room table centre.

BANISHING THE WINTER

After seeing this beautiful arrangement you are sure to be tempted to invest in a spring collection of your own. Once spring is on its way dried flowers somehow seem to lose their impact. Fresh colours and lively, vivid shapes are what people enjoy seeing at this time. (Autumn, on the other hand, is a season in which dried flowers almost invariably look appropriate. Their subdued colourings and soft outlines are very

A Trough of Spring Flowers by Monique Regester

much at one with the season of "mists and mellow fruitfulness.") Pack your favourite dried materials carefully away for next year, bring on a few fresh bulbs indoors and supplement them with a decoration using artificial materials of this sort, and the gloom of winter will soon be hurrying away. Remember that,

even if you cannot obtain or afford top-quality waxed paper flowers, you could use this arrangement as inspiration for one of your own made with polyester silk flowers. So long as the polyester silk versions are the best you can buy, your arrangement will have much of the charm of this one.

A Kitchen Swag of Fruit and Vegetables

This is another example of my own "homework", completed when I first went to work at Constance Spry's home at Winkfield. My job there initially was to work in the garden and, after a day in the open air, I liked nothing better than to wander into the workshop to see the staff making artificial materials. I learned a great deal from watching them create so many wonderful things, though I'm sure my own efforts must have caused them some amusement.

A Kitchen Swag of Fruit and Vegetables

In fact, large vegetables are not as difficult to make as the flowers and fruit shown earlier in this chapter, though they still require lots of patience, some modelling technique and an eye for colour. The basic shape is formed from a ball of cotton wool or polystyrene, bound round and round with narrow strips of crepe paper to make the desired shape. This is then hand-painted to give the background colour and dipped into melted wax of various kinds. The different waxes are used to give different effects and this part of the process is particularly skilled. Then the wax is scored and lined to imitate the surface texture of the fresh original, coloured to bring out these marks against their background and dipped in wax yet again to hold the colour in.

WORKING FROM FRESH ORIGINALS

Whatever you are making, from a cabbage to an asparagus spear, you must always work with the fresh vegetable beside you to ensure that the imitation is as close as possible to the real thing. The cabbage is made in two parts: the centre is made from a ball of cotton wool again, bound with paper, while the outer leaves are cut individually using real leaves as templates. These are carefully peeled away in sequence, numbering them as you go, and for each one a double layer of paper is cut. Then the veins and the thickening towards the stem are glued into position, sandwiched between the double layers of paper. Whatever fruit or vegetable is being modelled, it is the extra little detail that helps to make it more lifelike – the paper calyx fixed to the tip of tomatoes or the tuft of roots at the base of garlic or onions.

This description may make the technique sound quite straightforward, if a little painstaking, but in reality it needs considerable skill and experience, and the waxing in particular is not something that can be undertaken easily. I was lucky enough to have the help of a great many friends, in the true Constance Spry spirit, but you may be able to produce something very similar with a little "cheating". First of all, it is perfectly acceptable to use some real dried vegetables like the gourds and the garlic I have used here. These ornamental gourds are quite easy to grow yourself. Seeds are usually available in mixed collections and can be started off indoors, on a sunny window sill. Plant them out into the garden in a position that will afford full sun for as long as possible. They need to be supported and can be trained up trelliswork or fencing. The fruits are borne in the autumn and should be left on the plant to ripen. Once they are quite hard and the foliage on the plant is beginning to die off, harvest the gourds and leave them somewhere dry and sunny (a greenhouse is ideal) to dry out further still for several weeks. Before using them in an arrangement you can paint them with a clear, matt varnish to preserve their vivid colours.

In addition, you can use some of the plastic fruits and vegetables that are available from time to time. To make these more realistic, paint them carefully all over with matt paints to rid them of their unnatural shine and to bring out more of the detail of the fresh original. Don't forget to paint some dirt on to the root vegetables, too, to help with the realism. Finally, you should wire each of them up before mounting them on to the swag. Artificial grapes can easily be bought ready-made and these are so good that they can be used with little or no modification.

SHAPING UP THE SWAG

The swag itself is made from plaited raffia, though if your timing is good you may be able to pick up a discarded garlic plait from your greengrocer or delicatessen – particularly if you are buying the last few bulbs to include in your swag! Before you begin fixing everything in place, lay the plait on the floor and arrange the vegetables and fruit so that you are obtaining the right shape, tapering towards the ends and swelling out, forwards as well as sideways, in the centre. Then start to mount the material by pushing the wires carefully into the plait and tucking them well out of sight. You should start from the ends and work towards the fuller section in the middle, saving the dried materials to be glued into position at the end. To give you an idea of the kind of subjects you can use, my swag in the photograph contains beetroot, cherries, onions, radishes, aubergines, turnips, tomatoes, apples, oranges, garlic, asparagus, cabbage, dried gourds, carrots and grapes. Remember, too, to try to introduce a little foliage here and there to help the different materials blend into one another.

AN UNUSUAL CHRISTMAS DECORATION

A swag like this, or even a much smaller and simpler version, can look very effective as an unusual decoration in the kitchen at Christmas, and can last for many years if carefully looked after. Dust can be brushed off with a soft brush but the tops of the fruit and vegetables will collect a film of grease from cooking oils and fats, which in turn attracts more stubborn dirty marks. These can all be removed by wiping carefully with a soft cloth dampened with detergent or methylated spirits. If dirt becomes a real problem you could dip the entire swag into a bath of warm, soapy water, but this is rather a drastic solution and regular, gentle cleaning using the method described above is preferable.

Flowers just for Fun

Once in a while it is fun to break all the rules, and the arrangements shown on the next few pages do just that. The style is exciting and impressionistic, with clashing colours, exotic textures and not even an attempt at accurate imitation of a natural original!

The photograph on page 97 shows some examples of the kind of materials in this category that are available ready-made. At the back are some very modern black and white acrylic flowers made in Hong Kong to a design by Carto Collina from Italy. In the small pot to the right, by contrast, the beautiful glass tree peony is quite old. I brought this back from a visit to Japan many years ago, but you can still buy similar flowers made from this opaque glass. The golden rose is also something from the past and has been tooled with almost Fabergé-like perfection from a strong, metallic foil. The red rose next to it, on the other hand, is made entirely from wood and comes from Holland. These are becoming more and more popular and can now be bought in a number of different countries. The group on the left is a mixture of many different materials, including plastic, porcelain and even lace flowers.

Whatever you decide to include in a fun arrangement like this – and it really is a case of "anything goes" – you should still try to plan the arrangement carefully. Everything must be done by design rather than by accident, so to that extent you should follow the same guidelines as apply to any arrangement. With these materials, however, you can exercise unusual freedom in mixing colours, textures and subjects to create a stunning, decorative group.

Another approach you can try is to make the flowers yourself from ribbon, crepe paper and other basic materials (see the photograph on page 99). Ribbon roses, such as those in the front group in the photograph there, can be made by twisting and folding a length of taffeta ribbon around a stem which has been made from 18-gauge stub wire covered with green gutta tape. The ribbon is shaped into a rosette as it is folded round the stem and bound on to the stem with 36-gauge silver reel wire. You must be careful to continue binding each fold in the same place, not letting the flower gradually slip down the stem. For the leaves, use a cardboard template to cut shapes from some green flocked ribbon. For each leaf you will need two shapes, stuck together back to back with a fast-drying liquid adhesive and trapping a stub wire between them made from 7-inch (18-centimetre) lengths of 24-gauge wire. Bind the base of the leaf and down the stub wire with green gutta. A few small leaves should be used to form the calyx behind each flower and the rest should be mounted in groups of three or five on the flower stem. Veins can be traced on the surface of the leaves with a pencil.

FLOWERS FROM CREPE AND FEATHER

For crepe paper carnations, such as those at the back left in the photograph, choose good quality paper in bright pink or white. Cut the paper into long strips about 2 inches (5 centimetres) wide, with the grain running across the width of the strips. Cut along one edge of each strip with pinking shears and then cut half way across the strips at $\frac{1}{2}$-inch (1-centimetre) intervals, to create the frilled look of the petals. Take a 10-inch (25-centimetre) length of 22-gauge stub wire to form the stem and bend the end over into a short loop. Fix the end of some silver reel binding wire to this loop and then start to bind the crepe paper on to the stem in a continuous strip, wrapping the paper round the stem and binding it at every turn. Once all the paper has been bound on, taper the binding wire down on to the stem and cover with green gutta tape. Carnation foliage is difficult to make, so the stems should be left bare and the flowers used in a mixed arrangement containing other foliage.

You can also make attractive feather flowers, such as those in the front group in the photograph, for a modern collection but you must be sure to use good-quality, clean feathers. Each feather should be mounted on fine silver wire, twisted round the "stalk" of the feather and then brought back to form a double leg mount (see page 56). Using a stub wire for the stem, covered with gutta in an appropriate colour, bind on to it a small cluster of ready-wired pearls, or a similar suitable centre, using fine silver reel wire. Then begin binding on the feathers, starting with the smaller ones for the centre of the flower and turning the flower as you go. Use one twist of wire for each feather and ensure that it all stays in one place on the stem. When complete, cover over the mounting wires with more appropriately coloured gutta.

RECYCLING STOCKINGS

Another easy idea is to make flowers from brightly coloured tights or stockings, such as those in the group to the back right of the photograph on page 99. First you must prepare a wire for each petal from 10–12 inch (25–30 centimetre) lengths of 22-gauge stub wire, covered with white or natural gutta or coloured crepe paper. Decide how many petals you want for each flower (this can be as few as four or five, or as many as twelve) and then shape the ends of the wires round differently sized jam jars to give some smaller ones for the centres of the flowers and larger ones for the outsides. Each petal wire should consist of a loop with a stem. Then cut a strip from a pair of stockings or tights, about $2\frac{1}{2}$–3 inches (6–7.5 centimetres) wide. Cut along one side of the strip to open it out and lay it across the loop of a petal wire, pulling it down on either side towards the point where the end of the loop meets the stem and binding it at this point with 36-gauge binding wire, down on to the stem. It may be necessary to trim some of the material away at an angle here if it bunches up too much. Make up each petal like this and cover the binding wires with gutta. Make the centre from a ball of cotton wool covered with more material from the tights and attach a length of binding wire to its base. Assemble the petals round the centre one at a time, binding each one on with one twist of the binding wire and finishing by binding down the stems to join them all together. Cut away the excess wire and cover the stems and binding with gutta. Finally, shape the petals by gently bending and modelling the wire to

A Collection of Unusual Artificial Flowers

Making Crepe Paper Roses

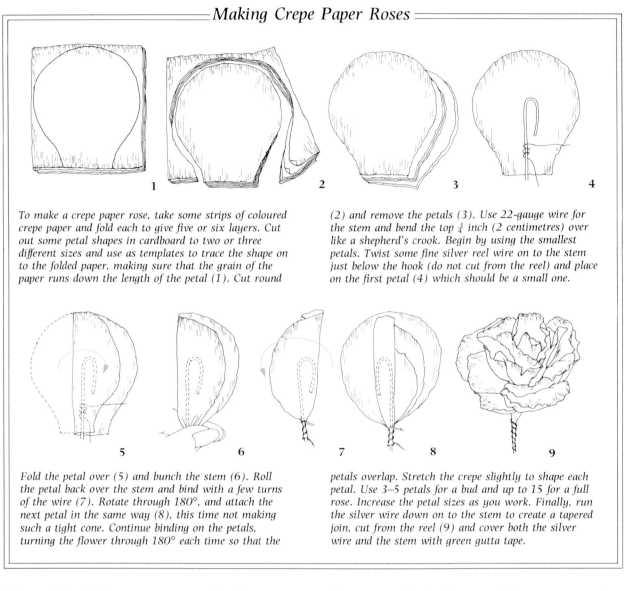

1   2   3   4

To make a crepe paper rose, take some strips of coloured crepe paper and fold each to give five or six layers. Cut out some petal shapes in cardboard to two or three different sizes and use as templates to trace the shape on to the folded paper, making sure that the grain of the paper runs down the length of the petal (1). Cut round

(2) and remove the petals (3). Use 22-gauge wire for the stem and bend the top ¾ inch (2 centimetres) over like a shepherd's crook. Begin by using the smallest petals. Twist some fine silver reel wire on to the stem just below the hook (do not cut from the reel) and place on the first petal (4) which should be a small one.

5   6   7   8   9

Fold the petal over (5) and bunch the stem (6). Roll the petal back over the stem and bind with a few turns of the wire (7). Rotate through 180°, and attach the next petal in the same way (8), this time not making such a tight cone. Continue binding on the petals, turning the flower through 180° each time so that the

petals overlap. Stretch the crepe slightly to shape each petal. Use 3–5 petals for a bud and up to 15 for a full rose. Increase the petal sizes as you work. Finally, run the silver wire down on to the stem to create a tapered join, cut from the reel (9) and cover both the silver wire and the stem with green gutta tape.

bring a little lifelike movement into the flower.

A few bulrushes can look very effective with a collection of home-made flowers like these and you can make them yourself from brown velvet material. Cut a piece approximately 4 inches (11 centimetres) square and fold it in half, inside out. Stitch along one of the short sides and down the length to form a bag and then turn it the right way out. Attach a wire or a cocktail stick to the end of a plant cane, cover with gutta and then insert it into the open end of the bag. Push the sharp point through the end of the bag so

that it protrudes by about 1 inch (2.5 centimetres), to form the spike on top of the bulrush. Then fill the bag evenly with kapok or cotton wool and stitch along the bottom of the bag to close it.

As you can see from the photographs, a collection of these flowers can look very effective. It is quite a good idea to mix them with a few dried materials, too, like the dried corn shown here, or with some polyester silk foliage bought from a florist or a department store. Whatever you choose to include, bright colours and fun mixtures are appreciated by old and young alike.

Crepe Paper Carnations and Crepe Paper Roses (above left); Crepe Paper Poppies (above centre); Velvet Bulrushes and Stocking Flowers (above right); A collection of assorted *"flowers for fun" including examples of Ribbon Roses, Feather Flowers, Foil Flowers and Tissue Paper Roses (below centre)*

CHAPTER THREE

LONG-LASTING FLOWER ARRANGEMENTS

Although the title of this book mentions arrangements made using dried and artificial materials only, I believe there are several good reasons for including the six "rogue" long-lasting arrangements you'll find in this chapter.

The first is that a number of dried, drying or artificial stems are used here in combination with long-lasting fresh materials, and the ability to mix and mingle materials in this way is an important and useful skill to acquire. You will often find, too, that a mixed arrangement of this sort works to the advantage of the materials themselves: top-quality artificial blooms, for example, can take in almost anybody when sensitively arranged with real foliage.

Secondly, the "everlasting" nature of arrangements made using exclusively dried or artificial materials is rarely either required or obtained; in practice, you'll find that you'll want to change and alter an arrangement after two or three months in any case – and many of the arrangements to be found in this chapter will last for this length of time without any difficulty.

Long-Lasting Orchids in an Upright Urn

The luxurious aspect of buying and displaying orchids is now a thing of the past: thanks to the rapid strides made in commercial orchid cultivation most of us now enjoy comparatively inexpensive year-round supplies of these beautiful flowers. I have visited an orchid farm in Singapore myself, and was amazed to see how readily these difficult plants grew in the strips of cleared jungle, much as cottage gardeners grow sweet peas in England!

In combination with the orchids, I have used alnus (alder): a favourite tree of mine. It has just lost its foliage and will slowly change in a warm room: the catkins will elongate and the young cones open, while the dark cones from last year will remain the same. At the centre of the arrangement are some handsome emerald leaves of berberis japonica, which help draw out the delicate yellow-green of the orchids. If the orchids are freshly purchased, the arrangement should last three to four weeks in water. Remember to check the water level in the vase from time to time, though; it will go down quite quickly.

COLOURS AND CONTRASTS

This is a very easy decoration to make and one that I believe would give pleasure in many homes. There is, in fact, no real need to worry about colour. You can get very similar orchids in white, which would look good in almost any environment, and, if you had the right background, some of the red orchids currently available could also be very striking. Ask your florist what's on the market because different varieties and shades come and go all the time.

Perhaps I should mention at this point the possibility of producing the arrangement using artificial orchids and foliage: there are some very good artificial sprays of orchids now on the market, and also some foliage like the berberis I have used, so you could combine both with the natural alder (which would dry and remain perfect without water). The use of artificial orchids would open up a new palette of colours for you to work with.

I have chosen a lovely green urn for this arrangement, but a modern cylinder or classic urn would also

Long-Lasting Orchids in an Upright Urn

be fine here. For a more rustic look you could try a watertight tin covered in straw or hessian cloth.

Fill the container with wire netting alone: you'll need a single piece crumpled up and going right to the base of the vase to give full support to the stems. Select three or four stems of alder, and position these first to establish the outlines of the arrangement. Take care that you get the cones and catkins in the right areas:

this is difficult to lay down exact guidelines for, but you will probably instinctively know when you find a successful combination, like that shown in the photograph. You'll need one upright branch for the back of the vase, one for each side, and something to come low over the front. Just a tip here: if the branch swings round a bit, secure it with a hook from a bent piece of the netting in the vase. It must be firm because the orchids have very thin, wiry stems and need a steady background to rest against.

Once the alder is in position, insert the berberis leaves. They make an important focal point and must flow well from the centre of the vase. Then it will be time to insert the orchids: around seven stems should be enough for a vase of this size. They, too, must flow freely from the centre point, the tips coming out into the tracery of the alder branches, and the front ones flowing well over the front of the vase.

Camellias for a Mantelpiece

As I mentioned in the brief introduction to this chapter, one of the pleasures of having a wide range of top-quality artificial flowers to draw on is that the possibilities for producing attractive mixtures using real/artificial combinations are numerous. This elegant mantelpiece arrangement illustrates, I think, how effective such combinations can be. The sumptuous, waxy camellia foliage is real, while the pink and white blossoms are artificial. The quality of these blossoms is improving all the time, but if your standards are very high you'll find one or two tips below for improving their finish still further.

The stems of fresh camellia foliage are extremely long-lasting, which makes their expense worthwhile. So long as you keep the water in the container topped up, the decoration should last a full six weeks before the foliage begins to drop.

MANTELPIECE CONTAINERS
Although this long arrangement would be well-suited to any narrow shelf, it looks particularly effective on a mantelpiece, as seen here. I have used a heavy mirror trough designed many years ago by Mrs Spry: it has a zinc lining, and bevelled mirrors are set one each side of its exterior. Its shape makes it ideal for a position such as this, and the mirrors help reflect and intensify the deep, cool green of the camellia foliage. A small piece of oasis is positioned in the centre section with a small unit of wire netting at each end, providing an ample water reservoir but also giving additional support for the fairly long and weighty stems of camellia from the netting.

At this point you have a choice. You may either fix the flowers to the stems of fresh camellia before positioning them in the vase (this is the only practicable solution if you mean to use a glue gun to fix the flowers to the foliage); or you may attach the blooms by wiring once the foliage is in position. I have used a combination of both methods for the arrangement we have photographed.

POSITIONING FOR A LIFELIKE FINISH
The most important point about this simple arrangement is that the flowering stems are positioned so that they look as if they have just been picked from the garden. This takes time, care and skill, and ideally one should study how the camellias grow in nature to really get a correct effect. One way of increasing the lifelike appearance of the camellias is to lift them off their plastic stems and glue them to dried stems of helichrysum angustifolium (curry plant), or anything else of similar thickness and malleability. This stem is then wired to the real foliage, and the overall effect is a much more realistic one than would be achieved with their original plastic stems. More details of this process are given below.

You can, in fact, use two types of flowers: there are the blooms fixed to foliages and sold as camellia plants for artificial flower arranging, but there are also blooms sold as milliner's supplies and used in hat and dress manufacture; these can, on occasion, be excellent. Those sold on the plant as artificial flowers do, in fact, need more preparation. Take them carefully off the plant and glue to a short length of false stem (see above). You may find that the whole flower collapses, but this is not a disaster; simply glue it back in stages, keeping the plastic calyx to hold the petals firmly. You may be able to hide the little false stem at the back of the branch and glue it out of sight. If not, it must be wired with a fine binding wire, and the wire then covered with a little gutta percha to disguise it. The dress camellias will already be on a little wire: simply bind this to the branch and cover with gutta.

The colours of many of the artificial camellias are limited and often unreal. You can get better results by buying white or soft pink blooms and then hand-painting them with well-thinned oil paints yourself. Remember that painting from life will give by far the best results, so try to find at least one real bloom to take as your model. Once you have achieved the correct colour and the paint has dried, you can dip

Camellias for a Mantelpiece

them quickly in a fine paraffin wax, giving just a light cover. Dry them straight away.

Grade out the buds and flowers, and fix a number to the foliage stems before you begin to arrange them, getting them to lie in a lifelike way on the branches. Fix the remainder of the flowers after the stems are in place. Position the stems carefully, making sure that the height is adequately and pleasingly set at the back of the arrangement, and that the stems flow well from the ends of the vase. Ensure that a number of pieces curve over the front of the vase and mantelpiece to break the hard lines that would otherwise distract the eye. Finally, add your last blooms, using them to fill any gaps or empty areas that may have developed as the stems were arranged. Once complete, the arrangement needs little maintenance apart from a regular topping up of the water supply: if the foliage becomes dry, the leaves will drop straight away.

Mixed Chrysanthemums in a Copper Bowl

Simple arranging techniques coupled with a stunning show of colour provide the keys to this most effective display. I was lucky enough to have the chrysanthemums given to me by one of my generous friends in London's New Covent Garden flower market, and I believe they are all home-grown. The more you examine them, the more you will appreciate their quality, and the range of colours is a genuine tribute to those nurserymen who work so hard to provide the rich variety of plants that form the raw materials of the flower arranger's art.

When you are buying chrysanthemums, always

take a good look first to check both their quality and their life expectancy. Single blooms should have a hard, green cushion of stamens at their centre with just a trace of yellow pollen around the edge. If the centre is soft and yellow, then the life of the flower is nearly over and you should be looking elsewhere. The colours I have chosen are rich, striking and all in the yellow-orange-red range that looks so good against a dark background, with plenty of polished wooden furniture and opulent velvety fabrics. There are many other colours available, however, and for a lighter, sunnier environment, perhaps with pale greens and yellows in the colour scheme, you might like to try creams, yellows and whites. You could, of course, try an arrangement like this in just one colour, but I think that's a shame when so much variety is

available, since a range of toning colours like that shown in the photograph has so much impact.

FOLIAGE FOR INTEREST AND CONTRAST

The foliage used here, apart from some of the chrysanthemums' own leaves, is bergenia cordifolia and eucalyptus. The latter makes fascinating foliage for flower arranging and can be obtained in two distinct forms. The first has small, often rounded leaves growing in opposite pairs on many-branched stems – you can see an example of this coming out over the table at the bottom left of the arrangement. The second form has much larger, more pointed leaves, alternately arranged on longer stems, and you can see these to the bottom centre of the arrangement. What makes these two forms so interesting is

Mixed Chrysanthemums in a Copper Bowl

that both appear on the same plant, the former as a juvenile growth and the latter when the plant reaches maturity after one or two years. You can cultivate a eucalyptus tree in your own garden, provided that it can obtain maximum sunshine in the summer and can be given plenty of room to grow. The variety most frequently grown outside its native Australasia is eucalyptus gunnii (cider gum), which has more rounded juvenile leaves than those shown in the photograph, and a colouring ranging from deep blue-green to silver-grey. The tree is very fast growing, reaching 15 feet (4.5 metres) in the first three years, and can reach an ultimate height of 45 feet (14 metres) in maturity. By careful pruning, however, this rapid growth can be kept in check. For smaller gardens eucalyptus can be grown as a shrub by cutting it back to within 1 inch (2.5 centimetres) of the soil in early spring every year, although it will only ever provide the juvenile leaf-form if managed in this way. The best time to cut stems of eucalyptus foliage for use in an arrangement is in winter, when the plant is dormant, as they will last three or four weeks after cutting at this stage.

PREPARING THE MATERIALS
Before starting to arrange the materials it is important to give the chrysanthemums a long drink, so that the stems are fully charged with water. Cut and split their stems and remove all the foliage that will not be required for the arrangement to prevent loss of moisture by transpiration from the surface of the leaves. Then stand the stems in a bucket of water for at least 12 hours, keeping the leaves out of the water and checking from time to time to make sure the water level is maintained. The eucalyptus stems should have the lower leaves removed and should be split at the base, while the bergenia should be cut at a sharp angle and again split at the the base of the stem.

The container is a round, flattish copper bowl with three brass feet. Into this a piece of oasis was set with a layer of wire netting over the top. The netting was secured to the rim of the bowl with oasis tape. The foliage was put into the container first, with the eucalyptus radiating from the centre in large, arching sprays, coming out over the front and sides. A few upright stems of foliage were also set at the back of the bowl. The bergenia leaves were placed across the centre of the vase, set as low as possible to hide the mechanics. In fact, it is quite difficult to spot them in

the photograph. The chrysanthemums were set in next, with their stems radiating naturally from the centre and with the darker colours kept low down in the centre, to give visual weight to the group. When arranging the flowers remember that this should be done simply and naturally. This is not an arrangement requiring too much artifice: drifts of colour and a pleasing outline will suffice.

GROW YOUR OWN
The number of different varieties of chrysanthemum available is enormous, although you will often find that they are only identified by colour and shape. If you do have the opportunity to choose named varieties, however, or would like to try growing them for yourself, any of the following should combine well in an autumnal group like this. Yellow: "Greta Vergagen", "Snapper", "Hoof Lane" (with an orange centre), "Yellow Tokyo" (spider-flowered) and "Regaltime". Cream or white: "Cassa", "Refour" (anemone-centred), "Snowdon" (double-centred) and "Tokyo" (spider-flowered). Apricot: "Apricot Marvel", "Remember" and "Delta". Bronze: "Dramatic", "Dark Lapana" and "Bronze Spider".

Growing chrysanthemums has become quite a specialist activity but keen amateur gardeners can grow their own flowers if they take the time to look after them carefully at every stage. They are usually supplied as "stools" (plants with all the foliage removed and the stem cut down close to soil level), which is the condition in which they should be overwintered, and should be planted out in rich, well-drained soil in late spring. They should be well watered once they have been planted and then left for three or four days before you resume watering. From then on they need to be kept well watered throughout the growing season. The young plants should be protected from the birds with plastic netting and as they grow they should be supported with bamboo canes. When they reach 6–8 inches (15–20 centimetres) in height, pinch out the growing tip to encourage the side shoots that will carry the flowers. You should also start feeding them with liquid fertilizer at about this time. If you want really large, showy blooms, then extra flower buds produced at the ends of these side shoots should be pinched out to leave one, strong bud. Once flowering is over the plants should be cut back to about 6 inches (15 centimetres) above soil level and the stools lifted out of the ground to be overwintered away from frost under glass in trays of compost.

This arrangement should prove to be very long-lasting, provided you choose flowers and foliage in prime condition and look after them properly. The room in which they are placed should not be too hot and dry (a cool hallway would be ideal) and the water level in the container should be kept well up all the time. With this sort of attention the arrangement could last as long as three or four weeks.

Wild Flowers from Southern Africa

As I mentioned earlier in the book, Southern Africa, and in particular the Cape Province, possesses a unique and fascinating flora. These specimens illustrate this magnificently, as I think you'll agree. I consider myself privileged to have seen them blooming in the wild. They are spring flowers, and as they originate from the southern hemisphere this means that they are available in September and October. Strictly speaking they could be called "semi-dried"; while they are not everlasting, they can be happily arranged and displayed without water and will last for several months like this.

Usually, they are sold in mixed, unidentified bunches. (As in this grouping, a number have generally been artificially coloured, which is a shame, as the natural colouring is so splendid.) The prospect of trying to identify each variety would be quite daunting as they are nearly all to be found only in Southern Africa in the wild, and few have successfully been transferred to garden or even nursery cultivation. Erica gracilis, for example, is the only South African variety of erica (heath or heather) to be available for greenhouse cultivation in Britain, even though I know of at least twenty-two varieties from the Cape. The bunches available from florists, and the groups often seen at exhibitions, usually include species like leucodendron, leucospermum, paranomus, mimetes and serruria (which are all members of the protea family), erica, melaleuca and brunia. One of the most dramatic of these is leucospermum, of which there are forty-seven species, but these are all nearly always categorized and listed simply as "pincushions" or "pinhead proteas". As you can see, exact identification is more a job for a botanist than a flower arranger, but I have done my best. You are, in any case, unlikely to be able to order single species by name and must be prepared to use whatever is available each year. The variety of colours and shapes will guarantee that whatever group you assemble the effect will be beautiful and dramatic.

HAPPY COPPER
The container I have used is another of my favourites. It is a polished copper bowl with small, round feet and its warm colouring seems happy with almost anything. I have used it with growing bulbs, cut spring flowers, berries and green foliage at Christmas time, and dried flowers in the autumn. You should always be on the look out for versatile containers like this to add to your collection, and open, bowl-shaped vases are often more useful than the narrow, upright ones so fashionable nowadays.

I positioned a piece of oasis in the container which had been soaked beforehand, and covered this with several layers of wire netting held in place with tape. I then cut the stems of each of the flowers and set them into warm water in a separate container for about an hour. Once they had had a good drink I started to arrange them in the copper bowl, adding $\frac{1}{2}$ inch (1 centimetre) of water in the base. When the arrangement is finished the water will gradually disappear and should not be replenished, as the plants will now last quite happily for several months.

COMBINING MATERIALS
The arrangement was made up like any other using fresh materials, first establishing the height and width, and then filling in the sides and centre. I have done it as a facing group but it could just as easily be all-round with the addition of a little more material (I used two of the market bunches). The three large pincushion proteas are leucospermum cordifolium and a species of erica has been used at the top and the left-hand side to establish the framework and set the height and width. On the far right there is a stem of leucodendron xanthoconus salignum, with its long sheath of narrow, yellow-green leaves around the flower head. Leucodendron coniferum can be seen in the centre of the arrangement, with pinkish cone-like flowers surrounded by pale-green, pointed leaves, while the similar plant with a spherical black centre,

Wild Flowers from Southern Africa

at bottom left, is probably leucodendron discolor. The female flowers are hard, woody cones which remain on the bush for several years, while the male flowers, borne on separate plants, fall off soon after opening. The lanceolate leaves around the male flower buds take on beautiful and varied colours just before the flowers open, however, and this is what gives such wonderful splashes of colour to the rugged Cape landscape in spring time.

Also included in the arrangement are several types of melaleuca, the plant with round, bobble-shaped flowers rather like young puffballs, while towards the top left there are a few phaencoma prolifera flowers, looking like pale-pink helichrysum with petals that seem to have been pushed back in the wind. Much of the remaining material is provided by further members of the erica family and you will find stems like these particularly useful in hiding the mechanics. My own ancestors travelled to this part of the world many years ago, and perhaps this is why I love these flowers so much and long to be able to return to see them growing in the wild again.

Mixed Fresh Foliage

One of the hallmarks of a genuine Constance Spry arrangement has always been the interesting use of unusual foliage. When Constance Spry herself first started there were many others who had made names for themselves arranging flowers, but it was her use of foliage, and the combinations of shape and texture she achieved with foliage, that caught so many people's imaginations and started a completely new style of flower arranging.

I feel Constance Spry would have approved of the vase I have used for this arrangement. This saucer-shaped vase on a tall pedestal lifts the materials and gives plenty of opportunity to achieve long, flowing lines down the sides of the arrangement. The vase is one from Constance Spry's own collection and was made for her by a friend in plain, grey porcelain. You could use any tall container but I think metal or ceramic would be more appropriate than glass, wood or basketware to show off the different shades of green to best advantage. It is also best to display the group as a facing arrangement and to place it against a plain, coloured background rather than a busy, patterned wallpaper or fabric. The colours are subtle and must be seen in simple surroundings if they are to achieve maximum impact.

PREPARATORY TREATMENT
For this arrangement, in which everything is fresh but will last for a long time if treated properly, I simply used some 2-inch (5-centimetre) wire netting over the top of the vase to support the materials. You can use oasis, however, and if you remember to keep it well moistened you may be surprised to find that some of the plants have taken root after a few weeks, and can be potted up to provide more fresh material later in the year. Whatever you decide to use, remember to prepare all the material properly, cutting and splitting the thicker, woodier stems and stripping off the lower leaves where they are not needed. You should also avoid very large, soft leaves like those of zantedeschia aethiopica (arum lily), which cannot take up enough water from the vase to replace what is lost by transpiration from the surface of the leaf, and soon become limp. The leaves should be fully developed, too, as immature material will not have sufficient strength to cope with the "hydroponic" (or non-soil) environment of the vase.

The first materials to go into the vase were the variegated phormium tenax (New Zealand flax) leaves at the back of the group. These established the height and were followed by some stems of eucalyptus leaves to set the width on the left and an iris leaf on the far right. Next I started on the centre with a stem of euphorbia hanging well out over the front (the semi-succulent greenish-grey plant just to the right of the vase pedestal), followed by the spiky dark-green leaf of helleborus foetida (stinking hellebore) with the ornamental cabbage immediately behind and above it. To the bottom right of the arrangement I used a stem of hedera (ivy), a leaf of aspidistra and a stem of symphoricarpos (snowberry) covered in beautiful clusters of snow-white berries. To the bottom left I used another stem of eucalyptus, together with a huge variegated leaf of fatsia with a stem of actinidia chinensis (chinese gooseberry) resting on it. These greenish-brown hairy fruits are useful in many kinds of arrangement.

Working backwards towards the centre of the vase I then set in the graceful, arching stems of green amaranthus together with a few green stems of cornus stolonifera (North American dogwood) and some rosemary. On the right I pushed in a large bergenia leaf next to the cabbage, followed by a stem of cyrtomium falcatum (holly fern) with its curiously holly-shaped "leaves" (more correctly called "fronds"), some stems of santolina and two stems of blue-green euphorbia (I used a slightly different variety here). To the right of the arrangement I pushed in a stem of nicandra physaloides (shoo-fly) with its unusual fruits carried inside a bright-green calyx. Two tall stems of cyperus alternifolius (umbrella grass) were set in to flank the two phormium leaves at the back, while another aspidistra leaf went in behind it. To complete the arrangement I inserted a single stem of iris seed pods and a single head of bupleurum in the centre.

FOLIAGE ALTERNATIVES
This range of different materials shows just what can be achieved with a mixed foliage arrangement. A wide variety of material is available all year round, and there is always something new to try. Provided you have plenty of variety and try to get the different shapes, textures and shades of green next to one

Mixed Fresh Foliage

another it is difficult to go wrong. Other species you might like to try include tradescantia, euonymous (spindle tree), olearia (daisy bush), hebe, osmanthus, ilex (holly) and elaeagnus. You can also use a variety of tree branches to give extra interest, such as salix (willow) and alnus (alder). One of my favourites for an arrangement like this is aucuba japonica (spotted laurel), which provides an excellent focal point, often bears attractive clusters of bright red berries and also lasts longer than most other large-leaved species.

A fresh foliage arrangement can last much longer than an arrangement of cut flowers, especially if it is kept cool and moist. Ideally, it should be displayed somewhere that is not too hot and dry, preferably out of direct sunlight, and it can work very well in a shaded passageway or a dining room that is only used infrequently. If you insist on including flowers in every arrangement, then you might want to include a few artificial blooms, but I would encourage you at least to try the foliage on its own once – you will soon see how effective and attractive its cool, soothing greens can be.

Mixed Hydrangeas in a Silver Wine Cooler

Hydrangeas are among my favourite flowers and this surprisingly simple arrangement is possibly the one I like most of all in the whole book (though I must admit the choice is a difficult one!). As a child I remember visiting the hydrangea walk below the cliffs between Ventnor and Shanklin on the Isle of Wight, off southern England, and I will never forget the breathtaking display of colours, from pale greenish-white and cream, to pale and deep blues, bright rose and beetroot red. They are very easy to grow – the number of plants which survive such dreadful neglect in so many suburban plots bears testimony to that – and look just as attractive in the garden as they do in an arrangement like this.

A COOL CONTAINER

The container is a large, silver-plated wine cooler and into it I set one block of well-soaked oasis. Over this I placed a large piece of 2-inch (5-centimetere) wire netting, with a single layer covering the oasis and the remainder bunched up around the sides to give extra support to the heavier heads. A little water was added to the base of the container – about $\frac{1}{2}$ inch (1 centimetre) – and then all was ready to receive the hydrangeas.

The heads used in this arrangement were collected from friends, together with a few from my own garden, so that there would be a wide range of colours. The colour depends on the variety as well as the soil type, but it is true that on alkaline soils most of the blue varieties will turn pink, while on acid soils some of the pink varieties may turn blue or purple. You can make these changes yourself by adding iron sulphate or alum (aluminium sulphate) to the soil in solution, but it is always advisable to cultivate varieties in their intended colours. Hydrangeas can be grown as pot plants and, with the intensive cultivation this allows, you can produce beautiful, large, richly-coloured blooms.

Some of the heads I used here were completely dry while others were only partially dried. In an arrangement like this, however, they will finish drying as arranged and thus provide a very long-lasting decoration indeed. A lot of the foliage should be removed – just keep a few leaves around the flower head to help draw up moisture to begin with – and the stems should be thoroughly hammered. Some of the heads I used were single, while others were in twos and threes on branching stems. To arrange them, simply mix them together so that the colours are intermingled, ensuring that adjacent heads are of varying heights. The stems should simply be threaded through the netting and pushed into the wet oasis. As it dries out it will become much lighter, but the wire netting will hold it firmly in place.

DRYING HYDRANGEAS

Once the arrangement is complete it should be placed in a fairly cool room so that it dries out slowly. If the heads dry out too quickly the petals (they are really papery bracts surrounding the tiny floret in the centre) become crisp and brittle. You can avoid this by adding a little glycerine to the water, but this tends to darken the colour of the heads and I prefer to try to keep their natural colouring. When the heads are completely dry they will last for a year or so, but you should not place them in full sunlight as the colours will quickly fade there.

Mixed Hydrangeas in a Silver Wine Cooler

THEMES AND VARIATIONS

Hydrangeas really are very versatile materials. As well as fresh and dried hydrangeas, you can obtain realistic polyester silk examples and even the plastic ones don't look too strange and unnatural. The blue-green polyester heads on the bottom left-hand side of the Flemish group on page 76 give a good idea of how realistic these artificial hydrangeas can be. You can use them effectively in more technical floristry work to produce items like wreaths, corsages or even a head-dress for a special occasion, and in arrangements they can be used singly in a mixed group or in greater numbers to act as a focal point for something larger. I think they look particularly attractive in a pewter container and I can picture quite easily an impressive arrangement you could produce based on six or seven heads in the centre of a large pewter urn. The other materials could include purplish-magenta gladioli, mauve carnations and dahlias, pink chrysanthemums, pink antirrhinums (snapdragons), and some deep-red prunus (ornamental cherry) foliage.

Another, more unusual long-lasting arrangement could be made using hydrangea heads in deep pinks and reds together with some bare branches of prunus spinosa (sloe) stripped of their leaves, a head of purple ornamental cabbage, an aubergine, a bunch of red grapes and some purplish "Lady Derby" carnations. These will all work very well together and should last two to three weeks. Those readers who have a copy of *Cordon Bleu and Constance Spry Entertaining* (Octopus Books, 1985) can see an arrangement of this sort on page 53.

CHAPTER FOUR

SEASONAL ARRANGEMENTS

Seasonal Arrangements

To be really clever and get the best from dried and artificial flowers you'll need at least four good collections – one each for autumn, winter, spring, and summer. It's best not to rely on one group in the same place for a whole year – people will get very tired of it and this is exactly the sort of thing that gives dried and artificial flowers a bad name.

The autumn group should be made completely from dried materials, choosing colourings to suit the room that the arrangement will be kept in. This could then be removed to allow for a large mixed foliage group in differing greens for the Christmas period. During Christmas week itself you could perhaps add red flowers (in which case you will have to make sure that the container chosen for this period holds water). The dried group could then go back for two to three weeks, after which it might be replaced with a

mixture of dried and artificial flowers – such as fresh camellia branches on to which hand-made artificial camellias have been wired, or, alternatively, natural rhododendron foliage, which is long-lasting, with artificial rhododendron flowers wired on.

A mixed group of silk flowers could then follow – forsythia, lilac, narcissi, tulips, hyacinths and soft foliages which these days come in good natural colour ranges. Your final collection could then be a group of silk flowers in summer.

Planning your arrangements in this way will show that you really care about your flowers. Even more important, it may also go some way to restoring the use of true seasonal flowers. It seems to me that this has been lost in recent years, now that nearly any flower is available year-round, world-wide, and it's something that concerns me greatly.

A Basket for Early Spring

Surprisingly enough, there are really very few flowers available for a genuine early spring arrangement. Gone are the days, thank goodness, when plastic tulips – as likely as not a free gift with a packet of soap powder – seemed to grace the front window of every other neighbourhood sitting room. At the opposite end of the scale, top-quality handmade flowers, like those featured on pages 88–93, are hard to come by and expensive to purchase. The polyester silk narcissi and polyanthus in this delightful basket arrangement, however, are just right. Even though you may feel that spring is the time to counter the cold, bleak days of winter with the magic of fresh flowers,

artificial materials like this can be a useful way to fill in the gaps, when one fresh arrangement has finished and a replacement has not yet been bought. You can cheat a little, too, hastening on the brighter days by bringing your artificial flowers out of storage before the fresh ones are freely available in the shops (at a reasonable price) or in the garden.

Any wide, flat basket will do, though as far as I know this particular handmade kind is unfortunately no longer available. The warm tones and country feel of the wickerwork go well with such a "natural" group, and the pieces of cork-oak bark used to hide the mechanics continue the rustic theme.

A Basket for Early Spring

To begin preparing the arrangement, I positioned an oasis posy dish at the back of the basket, offset slightly to the left so as not to coincide with the basket handle. Into it I set a small round of oasis sec, well secured with oasis tape, and covered with a single layer of wire netting. A little extra thickness of netting was provided at the sides of the posy dish and the netting, too, was firmly secured to the basket. Then I started to position the narcissi, making sure that the stems of adjacent flowers were of different lengths and that the three different colours of bloom were simply and naturally distributed. It is important not to set the stems in blocks, either by grouping the same lengths or the same colours together, as a much more natural look is achieved with gentle, rhythmical alternation.

Once the narcissi were in place a little bun moss was used to hide the container and the trailing stems of hedera (ivy) were threaded into the netting. The ivy helps make the line of the basket and connects the arrangement to its surroundings. Finally, the poly-anthus plants, complete with their own little collar of leaves, were placed along the front of the basket and any remaining gaps were filled with more moss and a few pieces of bark. If the moss is kept damp with a light spray of clean water from time to time it will hold its fresh, green colour and the polyester flowers will not come to any harm.

If you can find polyester silk daffodils these would work very well indeed with the narcissi, but I have only seen plastic ones, which are effective only when seen from a distance. The polyester silk polyanthus are as good as anything on the market and to add variety to the arrangement you could introduce some of the mauve and pink varieties that are available.

BROADENING THE SPECTRUM

To make an even larger group, you could also add some catkin-laden branches of salix (pussy willow). If these are cut before Christmas, placed in water and kept warm, the catkins will continue to develop. You can take them out of the water when they have grown into silver-grey, downy "buds", hang them up to dry and use them with artificial flowers in many different arrangements. Extra variety can also be obtained by mixing some fresh, early blossom with the artificial flowers. This might include hamamelis mollis (Chinese witch hazel), forsythia, jasminum nudiflorum (winter-flowering jasmine), garrya elliptica and chimonanthus praecox (winter sweet). These should all be cut when the flowers are just about to open, so that they last well, but you will have to devise a way of segregating them from the artificial plants in the container so that they can be kept in water. If you look out for them it is sometimes possible to find good polyester silk versions of some of these – I remember spotting pussy willow some years ago and forsythia is also sometimes available – but with a little ingenuity fresh and artificial materials can be mixed together quite successfully and you may be surprised to discover how difficult it is to tell them apart. As a bonus, of course, the winter sweet and witch hazel will add their marvellous scents to the arrangement, and these cannot (yet) be produced artificially.

Roses from a Summer Garden

There are probably more artificial roses available than any other flower. They are made from polyester, genuine silk, plastic, paper, waxed cotton, china – and even wood (see page 97). Some are very effective, particularly those in polyester or silk, and can even be mistaken for the real thing, while others are ghastly parodies of the natural original. One of the key factors here, and something you should always bear in mind when buying any artificial materials, is the colouring. Deeper coloration in the centre of the bloom graduated outwards to the lighter shades at the tips of the petals, or paler petals delicately tinged with colour along their fringes – this is the kind of subtlety to look for. Bright garish colours should be avoided at all costs – some of them appear to be unidentifiable new "varieties" that, thankfully, have never yet been produced in nature.

DISADVANTAGES OF NATURAL ROSES

Natural roses are not really long-lasting cut flowers, particularly if your arrangement calls for some fully opened blooms like those I have used here. A few varieties keep their shape well as they open, but most blow quite quickly and the colour of red roses in particular can deteriorate badly. Unlike many other flowers, roses go well together in a mixed group containing a wide range of colours. Unless you have an endless and richly varied supply of roses from your garden, then, there are excellent reasons for making up an arrangement of artificial materials to display throughout the summer.

The container I have used is an old alabaster tazza, a saucer-shaped dish on a carved pedestal. Inside the tazza I have placed a glass dish to act as a liner. Although a container usually needs no lining for an arrangement of artificial materials, this tazza is old and cracked, and quite likely to fall apart if it is handled too much. This is a useful tip to follow when preparing any arrangement destined to go into a delicate container – simply place the liner on a stand of the same height to ensure you get the proportions right and then set the dish carefully back into the container once the arrangement is finished and all the pressing and manipulating over. Inside the dish a piece of oasis sec covered with wire netting holds the stems in place.

The arrangement itself was made in the usual way. First the height and width were established with the longer stems, and then the framework was filled in with more long stems around the outside, working down from the top. In the centre it is important to get the more open blooms and darker colours set well down in the base of the arrangement to ensure that, visually, the "centre of gravity" is kept as low as possible. Finally, the gaps were filled in with roses at many different stages of development, from buds to fully opened blooms, and in a wide variety of colours. There was no need to introduce any extra foliage to hide the mechanics, as there was plenty on the rose stems themselves, but if necessary you can easily wire up a few sprays of rose foliage on double leg mounts to tuck in here and there.

Roses from a Summer Garden

As a general guideline for a large mixed group like this, you should try to introduce as much variety as possible by placing buds, half-open flowers and fully open ones next to each other, and by remembering never to place stems of equal length next to one another if you can possibly avoid it.

THE PRICE OF QUALITY

The price of good polyester silk roses like these can vary enormously, from a few pence for a small bud to several pounds for an open bloom with its full complement of leaves. You should always try to buy the best available, however, even if this means making a slightly smaller arrangement, as some of the cheaper varieties need a great deal of work to make them look realistic. The style and habit of the stem structure should be closely examined, for example, as some are much too short and unnaturally straight. These have to be cut off and the blooms rewired if they are to be really effective. Equally, the detail of the foliage and the inclusion of thorns all add up to a convincing replica of the fresh original which is well worth paying a little extra for.

If you are faced with a glut of roses in the garden and wish to try something like this with fresh materials, then the same sort of guidelines apply. Look for the most perfect, spotless blooms you can find, use buds and open flowers, alternate the lengths of neighbouring stems, and mix and match the colours as you please. Remember, though, that it is not quite as necessary to fill in all the gaps since these will soon disappear as the roses open out. When the petals fall they can always be collected up and dried for a potpourri (although petals fresh from the garden will be more sweetly scented), while the artificial flowers are carefully stored away to await the return of those long, hot, summer days.

Autumn Colours in a Copper Pan

The rich orange, brown and green colouring of this autumn group is wonderfully evocative of the warmth and ripeness of the season. Dried materials are the obvious choice for this time of year and the copper preserving pan complements their colours, as well as the autumnal atmosphere, perfectly. This antique container is one of my great favourites. Apart from looking right, it is easy to use because the wide, open top gives you plenty of room in which to radiate the stems. Any container of the same shape will do for this arrangement and if you can find one in the same lustrous, earthy colouring of this polished copper, then so much the better.

An alternative container you could use would be one of the heavy-looking, squat, round bowls that can be found in many florists' shops. These have straight sides and a wide mouth, and can be obained in dark green or matt black. A dark-brown willow basket would also work well. Remember that these containers can be used for fresh materials, too, simply by introducing a suitable liner. I always like to use an ordinary kitchen mixing bowl for this. Set on to a square of newspaper to avoid scratches these are perfect, especially if you can find one that just fits neatly into the chosen container. Some even have a notched rim at the base which helps to hold steady any wire or string you use to keep the wire netting in place. They might almost have been designed for flower arrangers rather than cooks!

For this arrangement I set half a block of oasis sec into the container and held it in position with a layer of 2-inch (5-centimetre) wire netting secured firmly to the two handles of the pan. The framework of the group was established first, using some of the larger stems of foliage. Sorbus aucuparia (mountain ash) was placed in first to set the height. The pinnate leaves give a most attractive background to the entire group, breaking up the outline and dappling the shadows behind the other materials. The width was dealt with next, using more mountain ash on the left, a stem of fagus sylvatica (copper beech) at the front left, and some pressed viburnum leaves on the right. All of the foliage used in this arrangement has been treated in a normal glycerine solution (see page 23). This is an excellent method for preserving leaves and the fact that it darkens their colour a little is not a problem for an autumnal group where dark, subdued shades predominate.

ORDERING PRINCIPLES

Once the main foliage was in place I looked carefully through the dried flowers and seed pods needed for the arrangement to decide on the order of working. Remember that straight, thin stems are easy to insert between the other plants, while thick and twisted stems are more difficult to manage without breaking them. The hydrangeas certainly fall into this latter category, so I set them in next, deep down in the container and coming right out over the front. These are among my favourite dried flowers — they look splendid when used on their own, as you can see from the photograph on page 111, while here they act as a link between the container and the rest of the group, crossing the dividing line that would otherwise exist at the rim of the preserving pan, and thus bringing arrangement and container together.

Autumn Colours in a Copper Pan

The tallest stem in the group was a seed pod of iris sibirica – a small, blue beardless iris rather like a miniature flag. Together with a few slightly shorter stems of the same subject, this was placed towards the back of the group. To follow, I used another long, straight stem, this time typha minima (dwarf reedmace). These were set in to either side of the tall iris seed pod, coming down the outer edges of the arrangement. I much prefer these smaller reedmace flower heads to the much larger typha latifolia (great reedmace, or "bulrush" as it is so often incorrectly called). The latter is harder to work with and there is always the danger that the velvety brown flower heads will mature and rupture, spreading thousands of tiny, downy seeds everywhere. If there is even the slightest indication of this happening, spray them at once with hair lacquer to seal the surface.

Next I put in the dried seedheads of the lupin. Again, these were placed to the back of the group, radiating down from the top centre on both sides.

Long-Lasting Christmas Foliage

These raise an interesting horticultural question for the flower arranger who also has a garden. Should you grow them for the fresh flowers or cut them for the dried seedheads? If you cut the flowers right back as soon as they are finished you will get extra flowers in the autumn, provided the weather stays fine and warm. If you leave the seedhead to develop, ripen and dry on the plant, on the other hand, this second crop of flowers is ruled out. Perhaps the ideal solution is to cultivate enough plants to have some providing extra flowers later in the season while others are left to develop seedheads.

PEPPER-POTS AND LANTERNS

The poppy seedheads came next. These attractive "pepper-pots" come in many different sizes, depending on the species of papaver they belong to, and their colouring too can vary considerably. Some have a lovely blue-green bloom to them and work well with pinks, greys and mauves, while others develop a warmer yellow-brown colouring and are ideal for the colour range used here. Be careful to choose the more natural-looking pods, however, if you are buying them from a florist, as some are available sprayed or dyed in the most garish and unlikely colours imaginable. Another useful plant is sisyrinchium striatum. This can be used for its fresh flowers or for the whorls of seeds that develop almost up the entire length of the stems. These were inserted next on the right of the arrangement – you may find them difficult to spot, as they are rather dark, but one can be seen extending out to the right just beside one of the cone-shaped seedheads.

Now it was time to thread in the graceful, arching stems of physalis (Chinese lantern). These popular dried seed pods are quite easy to grow – in fact, they can become a bit of a nuisance if allowed to spread unchecked – but it is important to cut them at the right time if the slugs are not to wreak havoc with the delicate orange membranes of the seed capsules. Remember, too, to hang them up by the leading tip of the stem, not upside down. Otherwise, when they dry, the lanterns will all be facing the wrong way! Other seedheads introduced at this stage came from a mixed bunch bought from a dried flower supplier. These varied and exotic materials are seldom correctly identified, but if you keep a look out for them you will be surprised at the increasing range of interestingly-shaped seedheads that are coming on to the market. Finally, a few fronds of pressed dryopteris (ladder or buckler fern) and some stems of berberis and viburnum were used to fill in the gaps at the base of the group and to hide all the mechanics.

Long-Lasting Christmas Foliage

Whatever your response to the cold, dark days of winter, Christmas is an excellent time to raise your spirits with some specially created seasonal decorations. I have included four different ideas on the next few pages, and I'm sure there will be something here to please everyone.

The first arrangement just uses foliage, berries and cones. Some people seem astonished that an arrangement without flowers can look so effective, but when you think of the wide variety of colours, shapes and textures obtainable from foliage alone it is really not so surprising after all. Remember that apart from the wide range of different greens you can find (holly alone would give you wonderful scope for a group of mixed greens), there are also browns, reds and yellows plus all the silvery shades of senecio and similar plants. Bare branches can also be used – think of rich red stems of cornus alba – and you can wire cones and berries on to them as required. Whenever I visit a public garden during the winter I invariably come back full of ideas, and the temptation to run riot with a pair of secateurs is hard to resist!

The arrangement shown here would be ideal for a sideboard or to decorate a buffet table, but its considerable size rules it out as a simple table decoration in all but the largest rooms. You can judge its height, which must be more than 3 feet (1 metre), from the 14-inch (35-centimetre) candles standing alongside. Consequently, it make sense to arrange it as a facing group, even though it could be done as an all-round arrangement. Always remember that an all-round group to decorate a dining table should never be too tall. Something much lower could be achieved along similar lines, however, if you started with a flattish, saucer-shaped vase and cut everything down by about half.

The container I used is a black, upright urn. The colour must be dark for a group like this, although you could choose from a wide variety of shapes and sizes. Into this I set a small piece of oasis, and then taped a layer of wire netting quite high up in the mouth of the vase. The oasis really only holds the first, outline stems firm – after that the netting takes over and the stems begin to support each other as the container fills up.

CATKINS AND SUGAR PINE
At the back of the group I placed a tall stem of garrya, with its attractive crop of catkins at the tip. To the right I used some branches of variegated ilex aquifolium (holly) and to the left some tsuga (hemlock or sugar pine). To extend the outer margins further still I used some stripped-back stems of sugar pine at the top right and top left, three branches of green cornus stolonifera on the far right and a single stem of hedera (ivy) on the far left. Once this framework had been established, I began to fill in the centre using holly-leaved osmanthus, mahonia, azara and the big speckled leaves of aucuba japonica (spotted laurel). A little cupressus (cypress) pushed deep down into the group was used to hide the mechanics.

The berries and cones add a particularly festive

touch to the arrangement. First of all, I pushed in some stems of cotoneaster at the back of the group – one can be seen at the very top, to the left of the garrya, while others are set down further to the top right. Next I used some berberis aggregata (barberry) at the top left and top right. The berries on these are not fully ripe, so their colouring is still yellow tinged with pink, but you can already see the waxy bloom developing. Some skimmia leaves and berries were pushed in next, at the bottom right-hand side of the arrangement, followed by another variety of barberry (berberis × rubrostilla this time) with lovely pendulous clusters of ovoid berries, placed even further down so that the berries almost touch the table on which the urn stands. The cones are of three types: larix (larch) stems bear the small cones that you can see at the bottom left and dotted around the group elsewhere, while the medium-sized cones at bottom right are pinus sylvestris (Scots pine). The long cones at bottom left are picea abies (Norway spruce).

A Christmas Mantelpiece

This is a very special Christmas decoration and the beautiful dining room in which it has been photographed is the perfect setting. A fire, especially if it is surrounded with a lovely carved wooden mantelpiece as this one is, will always provide the ideal focal-point at Christmas time. Topped with such a superb mirror, you can make a truly stunning feature out of it.

MAKING THE GARLAND

You should start by making the garland, but bear in mind that after about a week the foliage you use for this will start to look rather dry, especially if the room is warm and dry. This is inevitable in a centrally-heated home with a blazing fire as well, so you should be patient and make up the garland as late as possible before the Christmas festivities begin. First of all measure the length the garland will need to be with some string and then make up two matching lengths of damp sphagnum moss, each measuring half the total length. The moss should be carefully teased out and then either bound into a sausage shape with string or rolled up inside a tube of wire netting, packed in tightly to provide firm support for the wire mounts. The rolls should measure about 1–1½ inches (2.5–4 centimetres) in diameter and should finally be covered with a bandage of green plastic film. Fix the rolls up on either side of the mirror, securing them firmly but carefully at the top and sides, so that the garland can be made up *in situ*.

Now mount all your foliage on to 7- or 10-inch (18- or 25-centimetre) lengths of 22-gauge wire. Keep each different variety in a separate pile and divide the piles into two, one for each side of the mirror. Any evergreen foliage can be used as a background to the cones, berries and artificial fruits – cupressus (cypress), cornus (dogwood), laurus nobilis (sweet bay), ilex aquifolium (holly) and pine have all been used here. Insert the mounts into the roll of moss, working from the top downwards to the place where the bows will be fixed and then upwards from the bottom to the same place. Try to keep the shape reasonably regular as you go and get the foliage all facing in the same direction. Make sure that the foliage sits well down on to the mirror on the inside so that no reflection of the plastic-covered moss can be seen.

Now add the bows. These have been made up from sequin waste with strips of 1½ inch (4 centimetre) wide gold ribbon glued down the centre. They should be mounted on wire and pushed down into place on top of the foliage. Finally, add the cones, berries and artificial fruits, all mounted on wires. These come in a wide range of shapes and colours and are readily available around Christmas time. In the photograph you may be able to make out some real eucalyptus pods close to the two side bows (they look rather like acorns with a hole in the end). These come from my family's home in Australia and have been in my collection of dried materials for many years.

CENTREPIECE FOR A MANTELSHELF

The centrepiece on the mantelshelf is actually much simpler to make than it looks. The reflection in the mirror makes it look quite elaborate. Remember that the mirror will reflect everything, including any mechanics that are showing, so you will need to make sure the back of the container is neat and tidy before you

A Christmas Mantelpiece

start and that all mechanics are carefully hidden with foliage before the finished group is set into place. The container I used is an oblong copper trough, measuring 12 inches by 4 inches (30 centimetres by 10 centimetres) and 2 inches (5 centimetres) deep. Inside this I made up a stepped pyramid of oasis using three pieces of different lengths set one on top of the other. This is something I dislike seeing in an ordinary flower arrangement, but here it was essential to carry the plastic candle holders at different heights. Candles simply set into oasis would not be very secure and you need all the height you can get if the candle flames are to be kept well away from the foliage. The oasis was held firmly in place with wire netting and soaked to keep the foliage fresh.

The foliage I used included holly, ivy and pine, with some aucuba japonica (spotted laurel) coming out well over the front of the container. I also included some sprays of cotoneaster × "Cornubia", with its attractive lanceolate leaves and clusters of bright red berries. Finally, I added some artificial roses and lilies made from crinkle paper plus some pretty little golden apples made from tinsel bound on to balls of cotton wool. These are all mounted on wire covered in green gutta tape and should be dipped into varnish to waterproof them before being pushed into the wet oasis. Everything in an arrangement like this can be artificial, but do take care with the candles in this case, as artificial materials are highly flammable.

A Christmas Table Centre

The most important feature in any arrangement of this kind is colour co-ordination. Everything should be in matching colours and tones, from the artificial flowers to the cutlery and crockery. A white table cloth is one of the most demanding backdrops for any arrangement, requiring a great deal of interest in colour, shape and texture to make it really effective.

The container here is a low, oval dish in white porcelain, with gold bands around the top and the bottom to match the decoration of the place settings. A matching vegetable dish would work equally well. A small piece of oasis sec was set into the dish, held in place with a layer of wire netting.

A Christmas Table Centre

All the materials are artificial. Large fronds of different ferns, in gold and white, were cut up into smaller, more manageable pieces, and stems of holly, feathery white "hibiscus" flowers and tinsel sprays were also used. Everything was mounted on wire stems covered with gutta tape, including the bells and baubles, and you will be surprised to discover how far you can make your materials go with this kind of treatment. The wire also makes it easy to manipulate the stems into pleasing, more natural shapes. First of all you should set the outline of the group, working back towards the centre of the vase. The large baubles and the bauble "grapes" should be set in low down as soon as you have the basic shape of the arrangement fixed, and they are then held in place by the other stems as they are pushed in around them. Finally, bend over the wire mounts of the bells into graceful curves and insert them amongst the other materials to complete the decoration. Check the arrangement from every side, tidying any loose ends.

An Alternative Christmas Tree

I'm sure I'm not alone in believing that there really is nothing to take the place of a traditional Christmas tree, carefully dressed, as the highlight of any Christmas decorations. The Victorians certainly knew how to conjure up the festive spirit and this is surely one of the most enduring legacies of all from that age of plum puddings and Christmas carols.

Variety, however, is something every flower arranger should look for, and this alternative decoration has been created to suggest a different approach for some other corner of the house, where modern decor prevails and where a traditional tree might look out of place. For this tree the branch has been secured firmly using wooden blocks in a 10-inch (25-centimetre) flower pot to hold it firm and then tilted over at an angle of about 15° from vertical. The pot was wedged to hold it securely and then a small stack of logs arranged around the base to hide any sign of the container.

POSITIONING CLUSTERS

Once the tree is standing firmly upright it is time to decide where you are going to position your clusters of decoration. In each position you must attach something to hold the foliage. I prefer moss for this, although you could use oasis sec instead, but whatever you use it must be fixed to the branch quite securely. For the moss, tie some string to the branch where the cluster is to be set, and then bind a large fistful of teased-out moss on top of the branch – the technique is exactly the same as that described on pages 40–41 for the potpourri basket.

For the materials, select some large, dramatic fronds to give a bold outline to each cluster and to serve as a background to more delicately shaped sprays in the centre. I have used some huge, feathery fronds of cycas (Egyptian palm), together with mahonia branches, frosted pine and dryopteris (buckler or ladder fern), all made from a silvery, metallic material. There are also some large, translucent, oak-like leaves, silver baubles and a few sprays of silver, lily-shaped flowers. The larger pieces can simply be pushed into the moss or oasis, while the rest should be fixed with double-leg mounts made from 10-inch (25-centimetre) lengths of 20-gauge wire.

THE FINISHING TOUCHES

Once everything is satisfactorily fixed and arranged it is time to add the Christmas tree lights. I used quite a large set for this tree, containing forty individual lights, and it really does make a difference if you can make all the silver and glitter come alive like this. Remember to test the lights thoroughly before you begin – one bulb that has worked loose can give you hours of frustration once they have been installed – and then position them carefully, hiding the flex behind the branch wherever possible. Next I added some birds for a little additional interest. These are simple white doves, with their tails "dressed up" for the occasion. Wind some wire around each leg and then bind it on to the branch. Finally, I gave the whole decoration a touch of winter with some spray-on snow. Apply this carefully, keeping to one side of the tree only and using a piece of cardboard as a shield, to achieve the clean lines you see in natural, drifted snow. A bag of artificial snow poured judiciously over the logs finished the picture off perfectly.

An Alternative Christmas Tree

ACACIA

COMMON NAMES **Mimosa, Wattle**
FAMILY *Leguminosae*

A group comprising mostly evergreen trees and shrubs. Traditionally it has been most abundant in Australia, but is now scattered over many other warm parts of the world. *Acacia senegal*, a native of the Sudan, contains gum arabic (often used to glue seedheads) in its branches.

A few species are nearly hardy, and will survive a fairly cold winter if grown in a sheltered spot, but will need the sun in order to do well. Flowers appear from January to April as round fluffy balls of pollen in deep yellow through cream to white. The leaves are mostly bipinnate in juvenile form, later becoming reduced to a phyllode in some species. Acacia can be grown in pots, where they will form quite big trees, flowering well and needing little attention. They are often grown outside during the summer and then brought back into the greenhouse for protection during the coldest months.

TO PRESERVE: Hang up in small bunches or leave upright in a little water, where they will retain their graceful curved stems. Both flowers and leaves will keep well and hold their colour in a muted form.

RECOMMENDED SPECIES: *A. longifolia* (hardy species); *A. myrtifolia* (wall shrub); *A. riceana* (of weeping habit); *A. verticillata* (good under glass).

ACANTHUS

COMMON NAME **Bear's breeches**
FAMILY *Acanthaceae*

A native of the Mediterranean region, this is an easily grown perennial with interesting thistle-like leaves. Its name is derived from the word *akanthos*, meaning "spine". It will require a good sunny position to produce its white/dull rose flower spikes in midsummer. Coloured varieties will make particularly attractive herbaceous border plants.

TO PRESERVE: The coloured varieties in particular look very attractive when dried. Small leaves can be pressed. The flower spikes will air-dry well if hung up in small bunches. They are difficult to handle but well worth the trouble.

ACER

COMMON NAME **Maple**
FAMILY *Aceraceae*

Mostly deciduous trees and shrubs comprising over 100 species, many of which are native to China and Japan.

The field maple (*Acer campestre*) is a native of Europe. In their fresh state, maples offer a range of coloured foliages which are very beautiful when young and later again in autumn. Unfortunately, much of their colour is lost in their preserved form. The field maple is, however, excellent cut when in flower and before the leaves open.

The Japanese maples (*A. palmatum*), with their many varieties, are excellent in the garden, though many will need protection from cold winds in the early part of the year to stop the young growth being harmed.

TO PRESERVE: Press individual leaves and glycerine short stems.

ACHILLEA

COMMON NAME **Yarrow**
FAMILY *Compositae*

A group of perennial herbaceous plants that are well worth growing because they dry so easily and hold their colour well over a long period. There are many different flower forms, in white, purple and yellow — some short and others with flower stems of up to 5 feet (1.5 metres) in length. Many have flat heads of flowers which form a colourful disc and are excellent in a large group. *Achillea ptarmica*, var. "The Pearl", is very pretty in its double white form and can be used in many different ways — the individual flowers are excellent in miniature flower arrangements.

Achillea likes well-drained open ground with sun. It is useful both in the herbaceous border or in the cutting area.

TO PRESERVE: Remove leaves from the base of the stems, then hang the stems up to air-dry in small bunches just as the flowers come into full colour. Dry quickly.

RECOMMENDED SPECIES: *A. filipendulina, A. millefolium*, vars. "Cerise Queen", "Moonshine" and "Flower of Sulphur".

ACONITUM

COMMON NAME **Monkshood**
FAMILY *Ranunculaceae*

A poisonous herbaceous plant that is found wild in Europe, Asia and North America. The flowers and then seedheads will make useful dried stems if collected in the autumn. Aconitum will grow well in a partially shaded position.

TO PRESERVE: Hang stems to air-dry in freely-circulating air.

RECOMMENDED SPECIES: *A. napellus*

ACROCLINIUM ROSEUM
(see HELIPTERUM)

ACTINIDIA

COMMON NAME **Chinese gooseberry**
FAMILY *Actinidiaceae*

A vigorous climber with small creamy-white flowers which turn to a buff colour before forming hairy fruits about the size of a large gooseberry. The leaves, which press well, are an interesting shape, and are worth collecting if you have a plant to hand. The fruits are interesting to use fresh but do not preserve. The arching, twisting branches may well be useful in a dried arrangement.

TO PRESERVE: Remove leaves then press. Strip and air-dry branches.

ADIANTUM

COMMON NAME **Maidenhair fern**
FAMILY *Adiantaceae*

A large group of ferns. All are very decorative, yet many people avoid them because they are thought difficult. They are available commercially dried and also sometimes "bleached". There is even a polyester/silk variation on the market but as yet it has not been perfected — the colour is right but the size of the individual leaves is not true to form. Adiantum will press well if picked when the whole frond is fully grown. They need plenty of light but do not like direct sunlight. Ideally, they should be grown in open compost with no watering or overhead spraying.

TO PRESERVE: Preserve fronds with glycerine.

AGAPANTHUS

COMMON NAMES **Blue lily, African lily**
FAMILY *Liliaceae*

A South African perennial which does well in colder climates in a good summer, although if grown outside, the crowns must be well covered during the winter months. It flowers in late summer or early autumn. Smaller varieties are easiest to handle, but once the seed is set no flower stem should be missed from cutting because they dry well.

TO PRESERVE: Allow to stand upright in an empty container to air-dry.
   Individual flowers can also be preserved with desiccants: wire flower heads before preserving if wished, although this is not always necessary.

ALCHEMILLA

COMMON NAME **Lady's mantle**
FAMILY *Rosaceae*

A group of over 30 species of low-growing perennials native to the mountains of Europe. One of Constance Spry's favourite flowers, the sharp green colouring derived from its lime green calyx will go well in flower arrangements. Alchemilla requires open ground with good drainage. Its velvety, palmately-lobed leaves are most attractive, especially when carrying a drop of water at each point. Although it can be rather fussy in shape, it makes a good filler in arrangements. The flowering period is normally early summer, and if cut well, the plant may produce a late crop again in the autumn. Cut when the star-shaped flowers are fully open and before the plant shows signs of turning brown.

TO PRESERVE: Hang up or stand upright in an empty bucket to air-dry. Alchemilla will also take glycerine.

ALLIUM

FAMILY *Liliaceae*

A large group of bulbous plants including garlic, leeks and onion, which are distributed over the Northern Hemisphere. Many have flowers which are well worth growing. They may have a very strong oniony smell, but once cut and in water this tends to disappear. Chives are also included in this group, although they are so consistently cut back for their valuable leaves that they seldom reach flowering stage.
   The blooms of this family range from pale lilac to purples and pinks and appear in July–August. Some appear as enormous heads on stems up to 5 feet (1.5 metres) high. The dried forms of allium are excellent. All may be picked and dried when the flowers are open all the way round though perhaps the smaller species such as the small yellow *Allium moly* are easier to handle.

TO PRESERVE: Stand the allium up in a little water to water-dry: this seems to help the flower retain a more open natural shape than air-drying. But if you prefer to air-dry hang them upside down in the usual way. Take care to see that each flower has enough room to hang free, as the heads can easily get tangled together.

ALNUS

COMMON NAME **Alder**
FAMILY *Betulaceae*

One of my personal favourites, this genus of trees comprises about 30 species spreading widely over the Northern Hemisphere and down as far as Peru.
   These trees make excellent free-standing specimens but if they are going to be grown in a group and cut regularly, try to plant them in moist ground, where they should grow again quite rapidly. Branches will make useful background foliage for large groups. The small cones are also worth collecting – they can be wired up and used for wall drops and flower pictures.

TO PRESERVE: Preserve the branches with glycerine. Air-dry cones.

ALSTROEMERIA

COMMON NAME **Peruvian lily**
FAMILY *Amaryllidaceae*

These very useful lily-type flowers make excellent fresh flower arrangements, but blooms left on the plant may produce very attractive seedheads for drying. These are sometimes varnished to give them an extra dimension. The Ligtu hybrids make well-proportioned flower heads as does *Alstroemeria pulchella*: another favourite for its unusual red/green and brown flowers which go so well in autumnal arrangements. Cut when the seed pods are well formed.

TO PRESERVE: Hang up to air-dry.

ALTHAEA

COMMON NAME **Hollyhock**
FAMILY *Malvaceae*

An old-fashioned hardy perennial which went out of favour because of its tendency to develop rust diseases which cannot be properly controlled. At one time, however, it was a favourite florists' flower and there were special classes for it at flower shows. There are now new double varieties of althaea which seem to be gaining popularity and perhaps it will soon be back in fashion.

TO PRESERVE: Hang upside down to air-dry in full flower or leave to produce a seedhead, which will provide a useful shape for a display later in the year.

AMARANTHUS CAUDATUS

COMMON NAME **Love-lies-bleeding**
FAMILY *Amaranthaceae*

One member of a group of some 50 species of annuals distributed over the world. Its green and red drooping panicle with long terminal tail-like flower stems make it extremely attractive in both fresh and dried forms.
   For growing, amaranthus are treated as half-hardy and are raised early in boxes ready for a good growing season outside. They are, however, subject to frost and will need a warm summer to do well. By cutting out the growing point of a well-developed plant, side shoots will develop

to produce secondary flowers which, although not as large, will be most useful for smaller arrangements.

TO PRESERVE: Pick when the flowers are half-out, then remove all the leaves and hang the stems upside down to air-dry or stand them in a little water to water-dry, ensuring that the graceful weeping flowers keep their perfect shape.

RECOMMENDED SPECIES: *A. caudatus* – var. "Atropurpureus" (blood red) or var. "Viridis" (green).

AMMOBIUM

FAMILY *Compositae*

An Australian annual, similar to knapweed, which, in colder climes, is often treated as a half-hardy annual.

The plant consists of a rosette of leaves with thick fleshy stems bearing small papery white daisy flowers with yellow centres. If dried too late in their growing cycle, these yellow centres turn black. Harvest early in the summer before the flower is fully open to prevent this.

TO PRESERVE: Hang up to air-dry.

ANAPHALIS

FAMILY *Compositae*

A perennial herbaceous plant native to Central Europe and America, it has a silvery-white foliage and a low matted growth, from which stems of papery star-shaped flowers grow in midsummer.

Pick before flowers open fully. Leave the silver leaves on the stems that you dry. If you have left the flowers too long before picking and you find they discolour, the centres may be carefully removed with tweezers.

TO PRESERVE: Hang up to air-dry.

RECOMMENDED SPECIES: *A. margaritacea* (creamy-white flowers); *A. triplinervis* (pearly white flowers with white/silver leaves); *A. yedoensis* (compact flowers).

ANEMONE

COMMON NAME **Windflower**
FAMILY *Ranunculaceae*

There are some 70 species of this plant. All produce interesting flowers – mostly from perennial rootstocks – but it is the leaves and seed pods that are of use to the dried flower arranger. *Anemone pulsatilla* is the best for this purpose; small flowers of species such as *A. blanda* may be pressed for picture work. Although anemones give great joy in the garden, the same effects cannot, in general, be retained in their dry form.

TO PRESERVE: Press the leaves carefully to retain their fern-like tracery and air-dry the fluffy seedhead as soon as it is fully developed. Some also recommend lightly varnishing the heads to hold them.

AQUILEGIA

COMMON NAMES **Columbine, Granny's bonnet**
FAMILY *Ranunculaceae*

A very old-fashioned flower with fern-like foliage and striking blooms.

A perennial, it is easily raised from seed and will produce excellent seedheads which dry very successfully – cut them just as they start to open. The alpine forms are small but worth collecting. The flower stems cannot be dried.

TO PRESERVE: Air-dry the seedheads.

ARBUTUS

COMMON NAME **Strawberry tree**
FAMILY *Ericaceae*

A small genus of which *Arbutus unedo* is an interesting evergreen small tree, with many qualities to justify its being grown by the flower decorator. It has pleasing leathery dark green foliage, ornamental bark, pretty bell-shaped white flowers and edible, strawberry-like fruits. Although it belongs to the Erica family, arbutus will tolerate a calcareous soil and so can be easily grown.

TO PRESERVE: The leaves press well and will also take glycerine, although this tends to change their colour. Branches can be used ornamentally.

ARMERIA

COMMON NAMES **Thrift, Sea pink**
FAMILY *Plumbaginaceae*

Wild forms of *Armeria maritima* are common by the sea. New forms come in a wide range of colours and with large flower heads. Easily grown from seed, this hardy perennial plant is well worth growing for drying. Pick the flowers before they are fully open.

TO PRESERVE: Hang up to air-dry.

ARTEMISIA

FAMILY *Compositae*

This group includes many aromatic plants such as tarragon and wormwood. Most are perennial and all appear to air-dry well. None have flowers of any great value but the foliage is most useful.

TO PRESERVE: Hang up to air-dry.

RECOMMENDED SPECIES: *A. abrotanum* (southernwood); *A. absinthium* (wormwood); *A. ludoviciana* (var. "Silver Queen"); *A. dracunculus* (tarragon); *A. vulgaris* (mugwort).

ASTILBE

FAMILY *Saxifragaceae*

This summer-flowering plant is not often seen in its dried form, but is well worth trying to keep for winter decoration. It is available in white, pink and wine-red blooms. The *Aruncus* which is allied to the astilbe is also worth trying. These plants may be raised from seed, but will need moisture and partial shade.

TO PRESERVE: The foliage presses well; the flower plumes are best dried in a desiccant because they tend to shrink to nothing if dried slowly in the air.

ASTRANTIA

COMMON NAMES **Starwort, Masterwort**
FAMILY *Umbelliferae*

An old-fashioned, easily grown perennial plant that is very useful for dried flower arrangements.

Some of the new varieties with strong colouring are in particular well worth growing. Found in the wild in many parts of the world, the flowers almost look dried when in their fresh state. Astrantia will spread quickly when grown in damp soil and partial shade.

TO PRESERVE: The flowers may be dried in sand or hung up to air-dry. They can, alternatively, be stood upright in a little water to water-dry slowly, although I find this tends to make them droop a little, unless the stems are kept short.

ATRIPLEX

COMMON NAMES **Red mountain spinach, Orache**
FAMILY *Chenopodiaceae*

The annual *Atriplex hortensis rubra* is worth growing but once allowed to seed freely it must be controlled, otherwise you will never be free of it. It is quite hardy and if sown early a good crop of stems 4–5 feet (1.2–1.5 metres) tall can be achieved by late summer. Other forms have grey foliage but the red is the most useful to the arranger.

TO PRESERVE: Hang up to dry when the fully coloured seed spike has developed.

AUCUBA JAPONICA

COMMON NAME **Spotted laurel**
FAMILY *Cornaceae*

A shrub that is often maligned but I think well worth having. Its foliage makes a useful year-round centre to an arrangement.

TO PRESERVE: Press or preserve stems in glycerine.

BALLOTA

FAMILY *Labiatae*

A group of mostly perennial herbs native to the Mediterranean region. Its silver-grey felty stem and unusual flower formation make it an interesting plant to dry. It is best to cut when young – the leaves and stems will then remain white. As it gets older they may become grey or fawn.

TO PRESERVE: Lay flat or hang up to air-dry.

RECOMMENDED SPECIES: *B. pseudodictamnus.*

BERGENIA

COMMON NAME **Elephant's ears**
FAMILY *Saxifragaceae*

These leaves are essential for any large arrangement as they are so useful for hiding the mechanics well down in the centre of the group.

TO PRESERVE: The large young leaves will take glycerine. Smaller leaves can be pressed and used in their dry state. When pressing, it may be well worth trying to get some of the highly coloured autumn leaves (do not use glycerine because the leaf will not absorb the liquid).

CALLUNA

COMMON NAME **Heather**
FAMILY *Ericaceae*

Numerous forms of this plant are in cultivation, ranging in colour from white to dark crimson.

TO PRESERVE: Pick when the flowers are in full bloom. Treat by placing in a mixture of glycerine and water or spray with a little hair lacquer before hanging up to air-dry. It becomes brittle when fully dry.

CAMELLIA

FAMILY *Theaceae*

A most useful foliage, which under normal situations lasts well when cut but will last even longer if treated with glycerine or pressed. *Camellia japonica*, with its fine, glossy leaves, is a particularly attractive example, making an excellent backing foliage for a large group. The flowers are extremely beautiful and you may be lucky enough to manage to preserve some with silica gel, but it is a difficult job.

TO PRESERVE: Press foliage, or preserve in glycerine.

CAPSICUM

COMMON NAMES **Pepper, Cayenne, Paprika, Chili**
FAMILY *Solanaceae*

Capsicums should be grown as annuals but started early to provide a long growing season. They produce small, round and pointed fruits in yellow, orange and red colours.

TO PRESERVE: The fruit should be allowed to colour up well before the plant is lifted and air-dried. Individual fruits may be cut off and dried separately. The fruit coats may be painted with varnish to lessen the degree to which they shrink.

CAREX

COMMON NAME **Sedge**
FAMILY *Cyperaceae*

A group of interesting grasses with tiny flowers and seedheads that are worth drying.

TO PRESERVE: Cut before fully mature. The triangular stems of these grasses may well give problems when tying them up to air-dry. The seedheads should be air-dried – they colour up from greys to gold and brown. Some may be stood up but I find if you can secure them, it is better to hang them upside down to keep the stems and leaf tips straight.

CATANANCHE CAERULEA

COMMON NAME **Cupid's dart**
FAMILY *Compositae*

A popular dried flower which is sometimes available in its fresh state. The flowers can be blue, white, yellow and bluish-white, and the seed box, with its several papery forms, is also of great interest for dried flower arrangements. In colder climes, it is grown as an annual and requires some time to get established.

TO PRESERVE: The flowers may be dried in silica gel.

CELASTRUS

FAMILY *Celastraceae*

A most decorative family of twining shrubs, in particular *Celastrus orbiculatus*, which is a splendid cover plant. Attractively coloured foliage in the autumn (which unfortunately cannot be preserved) is followed by fascinating decorative fruit heads in scarlet and yellow, which will dry beautifully on the branches.

TO PRESERVE: Cut side branches and shoots from the main stem when the leaves have dropped, and air-dry. The berry-like fruits will open as they dry. If wished, these can be immediately incorporated in an arrangement and they will develop in the vase.

CELOSIA

COMMON NAMES **Cockscomb, Prince of Wales feather**
FAMILY *Amaranthaceae*

These plants, native to the warmer countries of the world, will require a good summer to do well. Celosia are treated as half-hardy annuals and at the end of the season will produce large feathery plumage or a solid mass of flowers in a shape not unlike a cock's comb. They will lose some of their bright colouring when dried but will still be useful in their red and gold shades.

TO PRESERVE: Pick for air-drying just before they start producing their black seeds. They can also be preserved using glycerine, and smaller side shoots can be dried in desiccants.

CENTAUREA

COMMON NAMES **Knapweed, Cornflower**
FAMILY *Compositae*

There are many species in this family, covering both cultivated plants and weeds. The larger forms look something like thistles, to which they are related. The group includes annuals, biennials and perennials. Some have large excellent calyxes which dry well, but the buds are also interesting and may be varnished. *Centaurea macrocephala* is a striking perennial plant with rather poor yellow flowers but is well worth growing for its calyx. *C. moschata*, var. "Sweet Sultan" is grown as a cut flower. Its blooms, which resemble large cornflowers, come in yellows, whites and purples, and are worth drying.

TO PRESERVE: Buds should be air-dried and then varnished. Flowers may be hung up to air-dry, or may even dry on the plant in a warm summer.

CHOISYA

COMMON NAME **Mexican orange**
FAMILY *Rutaceae*

The evergreen shrub *Choisya ternata* is useful for both its leaves and flowers in fresh flower arrangements, but can also be preserved for use out of season, although glycerine may cause the leaves to change colour slightly.

TO PRESERVE: Mature leaves press well and also take up glycerine. Use silica gel for the flowers.

CHRYSANTHEMUM

FAMILY *Compositae*

Very few of the chrysanthemum family dry well, but as they are generally available all the year round this hardly matters much. The little button types such as *Chrysanthemum parthenium*, though, seem to air-dry quite successfully.

TO PRESERVE: Remove the leaves and hang them up in warm, freely-circulating air to air-dry.

CLARKIA

FAMILY *Onagraceae*

An easily grown favourite. This annual is a regular in many borders, and given sunlight will provide an excellent display – some growers like to sow it in the autumn to get an early crop for cutting the next summer. The flowers are normally a pinkish or mauvish white and appear in single and double forms, though new strains are always coming into the seed catalogues. Clarkia are excellent as cut flowers and also for drying. They are easy to handle and last well, retaining their colour. The seedheads, too, will make decorative additions to dried flower arrangements.

TO PRESERVE: Pick when a number of flowers are out on the stem and hang upside down or lay flat on slatted shelves to air-dry.

CLEMATIS

FAMILY *Ranunculaceae*

There are many different sizes and colours of clematis available today. The smaller forms, such as *Clematis montana*, and double forms are best for preserving, while the large flowered forms produce excellent seedheads: I dip the heads in varnish and allow them to dry quickly. The wild clematis is also useful but must be gathered when it is just becoming fluffy. It will need very careful storing to keep it in good order.

TO PRESERVE: Use silica gel to dry the small-flowered and double forms; air-dry seedheads quickly in warm air then coat them well with varnish.

CROCOSMIA

FAMILY *Iridaceae*

This orange flower is not unlike a giant freesia in its shape, but the stem and foliage are rather more reminiscent of gladioli in size. The seedheads are particularly useful.

TO PRESERVE: Collect seedheads as soon as the last flower fades. Hang them up to dry, and save a few of the better leaves to press. You may varnish the seedheads.

CULTIVATED GRASSES

FAMILY *Gramineae*

A large informal grouping that includes many genera such as wheat (*Triticum*), oats (*Avena*), barley (*Hordeum*) and rye (*Secale*). All are excellent and should be included in your dried materials. Ask a local farmer to allow you to pick specimens from around the edge of fields.

CYNARA SCOLYMUS

COMMON NAME **Globe artichoke**
FAMILY *Compositae*

This perennial herbaceous plant is a native of the Mediterranean area. The flower heads are very useful for drying, as are the young leaves which are ideal for small groups.

TO PRESERVE: Cut the flower head just as it is opening and hang upside down to air-dry. The drying may take some time as there will be a lot of stem tissue to dry out. Leaves may be pressed.

CYTISUS

COMMON NAME **Broom**
FAMILY *Leguminosae*

The deciduous bare branches of this common shrub are useful for giving clean outlines to a large arrangement. The long dark green stems may be used fresh or air-dried. Some people like to tie stems up into interesting, twisted shapes when they are still fresh and pliable, then, when dried, to use these to give special detail to a modern design. For the best results, use young new growth. From certain varieties such as *Cytisus praecox* (Warminster broom) some of the larger silver or green forms may also have their foliage pressed. Wild broom (*C. scoparius*) makes a useful source of supply.

TO PRESERVE: Air-dry young new stems, and press foliage of *C. praecox*.

DAHLIA

FAMILY *Compositae*

These are wonderful summer flowers for a garden display, but they are not ideal from a florist's point of view because they bruise so easily. They can be dried with careful handling but this should only be attempted on small flowered varieties.

TO PRESERVE: Pick each flower when it is nearly fully open and wire the short stem carefully. Then lay the flower head, stem end down, on silica gel crystals and dust carefully all over. Keep it like this for three to four days, then test to see if the petals have become papery. It's worth trying dry sand as an alternative because this is much cheaper to use, but do make sure that the flowers and sand are really dry before you start. If the sand is damp, or there is moisture deep down in the base of the petals, these will go brown and rot before they start to dry.

DATURA STRAMONIUM

COMMON NAME **Thorn apple**
FAMILY *Solanaceae*

A great favourite of mine. I first came across thorn apple growing as an annual in cut flower borders, and other varieties of datura in conservatories where their strongly scented white trumpet-shaped flowers can perfume a whole area on a warm evening. Unfortunately, it is only the prickly tulip-shaped seed pods of the thorn apple which can be used out of season. These are excellent in a big arrangement, but remember that they are extremely poisonous.

TO PRESERVE: Cut and air-dry stems bearing seed pods in an upright position.

DELPHINIUM

FAMILY *Ranunculaceae*

Most people are familiar with this flower in its annual and perennial forms. With its majestic flower spikes now available in virtually every colour imaginable, it is one of the leading herbaceous border plants. Some of the new apricot-orange varieties that are around are stunning, yet I still find the blues, mauves, pale pinks, creams and whites more pleasing.

Delphiniums make particularly useful dried materials since they provide both seedheads and flower heads for drying, and leaves for pressing.

TO PRESERVE: The flower spikes should be dried quickly by hanging upside down to air-dry in an airy cupboard, provided it is high enough to take the stems, which are 4–5 feet (1.2–1.5 metres) tall. Press individual leaves, which may be very detailed in shape, then wire and fix to stems. Collect seed pods towards the end of the season, then begin to air-dry standing vertically, allowing the seed to ripen so as not to waste it. Collect the seed, then hang upside down to finish air-drying. The side shoots or secondary flowers which may well appear in a good autumn may be cut again and these smaller heads can be air-dried across airing cupboard shelving. Individual flowers can be dried in sand or silica gel – these can be first wired and then, when dried, will work beautifully in low table decorations.

DICTAMNUS

COMMON NAMES **Burning bush, Gas plant**
FAMILY *Rutaceae*

This flower is not commonly grown, but is well worth considering for its unusual star-shaped seed pods at the end of the season. (The white or rose-coloured flower spikes give off a volatile oil when old which may be easily ignited on a warm, still evening – hence its common name.) Dictamnus is a perennial which does best in a dry warm area.

TO PRESERVE: Collect seedheads at end of season.

DIGITALIS

COMMON NAME **Foxglove**
FAMILY *Scrophulariaceae*

A great favourite in the wild, woodland garden. Digitalis now comes in most attractive colours which look very effective arranged in a simple vase with mixed early summer flowers. The seedheads dry easily and all varieties provide elegant slender spikes for a winter arrangement.

TO PRESERVE: Collect the seedheads at the end of the season, and rub the dead shrivelled "fingers" (the old flower heads) off to leave the seed pods on the stem. Stand them upright to air-dry fully.

DIPSACUS

COMMON NAME **Teasel**
FAMILY *Dipsaceae*

Most of us have come across these common wild flowers at some time in our lives. Although unpleasant to handle, the teasel is well worth collecting when the pale lilac flower is just finishing and before the seedhead starts to colour. (I have heard that if they are picked before the flower comes out, the immature head is a much better colour when dried.) Use them only in their natural form – those normally on sale have often been dipped or sprayed in very unnatural colours.

TO PRESERVE: Rub off the spikes from the stem and remove the leaves before hanging them up to air-dry. (A word of warning: when dry, the heads will seem even more spiteful to deal with than when fresh!) Teasels are very hardwearing and the seedheads will become very dark as they age. When picking them, it's worth separating side shoots from the main stems. These side shoots will be useful for smaller arrangements, and will also make the main stems more manageable to handle when hanging up to dry.

ECHINOPS

COMMON NAME **Globe thistle**
FAMILY *Compositae*

This thistle-like plant is common over Europe and Asia. It comes in both biennial and perennial forms: both have globe-like flowers in white or steel blue.

TO PRESERVE: Pick when the flower is still in bud – this is a point to watch carefully because it is not always easy to see from a distance. Remove the bottom leaves but leave the two or three nearest to the flower, as these will dry into a good silver colour. Hang upside down to air-dry. Pick only when the bud is dry.

ELAEAGNUS

FAMILY *Elaeagnaceae*

The name of a useful group of shrubs and small trees. A number of them have excellent silver/green and yellow/green foliage which is very long-lasting in water. Some also have edible fruit, although these cannot be preserved. It is their beautiful leaf markings, however, that earn them a mention here.

Elaeagnus leaves will press and dry very well, in many cases retaining their silver backs, as in *Elaeagnus macrophylla*, and the wonderful gold, green and yellow markings on *E. pungens* var. "Aureo-Variegata". These splendid leaves can be wired up on to false stems to make a stunning background for an arrangement. Press some in natural short sprays and others singly.

TO PRESERVE: Press leaves to dry.

EPILOBIUM

COMMON NAMES **Firewood, Willow-herb**
FAMILY *Onagraceae*

I have always found this plant when in flower very beautiful against the mountain background in Switzerland, and I know that Constance Spry loved it for its striking effect when used with certain reds. She used to strip off all the foliage and dip the stems into boiling water to make them last and keep their colour. I have never encouraged epilobium to produce seedheads in the past as it can be a nuisance if it gets established in the garden. Now I am having to change my mind, however. Once the flowers have passed, the seedheads curl. This is when you should cut them, and varnish the pods quickly before they split.

TO PRESERVE: As above.

EPIMEDIUM

FAMILY *Berberidaceae*

This is an excellent ground cover plant with attractive, though short-lived, flowers which appear in late spring/early summer. It is the leaves that are its most interesting feature. These come on long wiry stems and are leathery and interesting in shape.

TO PRESERVE: The leaves will colour up beautifully in late summer and early autumn and should then be pressed. They tend to curl naturally so time must be taken to get them well positioned under the paper so that they will come out flat and undamaged.

ERICA

COMMON NAME **Heather**
FAMILY *Ericaceae*

A very large group of evergreen shrubby plants widely dispersed over Africa and Europe.

TO PRESERVE: Hang to air-dry upside down. Some people like to spray them lightly with hair lacquer to stop them falling apart when they dry and become brittle.

ERYNGIUM

FAMILY *Umbelliferae*

Eryngium provides some wonderful plant material for drying with similarities to the teasel and globe thistle, but with strikingly coloured stems. They have a bluish inflorescence which carries into some of the foliage and flower stems. Eryngium is often grown as a commercial crop and will do well in the garden in a sunny position in fairly light and well-drained soil.

TO PRESERVE: Harvest when full of colour. If they are left on the plant too long, this will fade. Hang to air-dry.

RECOMMENDED SPECIES: *E. amethystinum, E. alpinum* and *E. creticum*.

EUCALYPTUS

COMMON NAME **Gum tree**
FAMILY *Myrtaceae*

Where would we be without this foliage plant today? Years ago only one or two varieties were occasionally available. Now, with the widespread introduction of hardy varieties, we have a range of different-shaped blue-grey foliages to add interest to our dried groups. Juvenile and adult foliages vary but *Eucalyptus gunnii* and *E. globulus* are two of the most important varieties. Some of the small-leaved varieties are quite charming – one in particular, *E. polyanthemus* var. "Silver Dollar", is widely available today and is excellent.

Although the trees grow very large once established, they will stand hard cutting back, which gives a ready supply of new shoots. The top of the trees may be killed by frost in a very hard winter: cut back to the main stem 2–3 feet (61–91 centimetres) from the ground and new shoots will soon grow.

TO PRESERVE: Air-dry or use glycerine to preserve branches and foliage. Little seed pods may be produced by some species, and these can be varnished.

EUPATORIUM

FAMILY *Compositae*

These flat flower heads on strong upright stems can be dried, having first stripped all the leaves, by just hanging upside down to air-dry.

TO PRESERVE: As above.

FERNS

A huge group of plants comprising some 10,000 different species in many different families. In the main I would suggest that they are carefully pressed, though some may take glycerine. Air-drying is inappropriate for delicate ferns as it makes the fronds curl up badly and completely lose their shape. These delicate ferns must always be pressed. Some ferns, though, are quite strong, like *Arachniodes adrantiformis* (the American leather leaf fern). This can be air-dried slowly without it curling up. I have another interesting strong fern, *Cyrtomium falcatum* (Japanese holly fern) in my own garden which never grows large. I use it regularly in fresh mixed foliage arrangements, and it, too, can be air-dried. Compound fronds can often be split up into small leaflets, which can prove useful when the whole frond is too large. *Osmunda regalis* var. "Palustris" is another fern that comes to mind as being suitable for preservation – the full frond is perhaps 4 feet (1.2 metres) long but the side leaflets range from 4–12 inches (10–30 centimetres) and these will dry beautifully. I usually put them under the carpet between layers of newspaper be-

cause they are too large to handle in any press. Some people presume that the general wear and tear of people passing over them soon breaks them up, but I have done it for many years with no detrimental effects.

TO PRESERVE: Press or air-dry as described above. Glycerine may also be used on *Cyrtomium falcatum*, or on side shoots of *Osmunda regalis*.

GALIUM

COMMON NAMES **Goose grass, Bedstraw**
FAMILY *Rubiaceae*

Although members of this family are weeds, they do have some good properties. The stems of the main plants are square and bear very delicate yellow and white flowers. Harvest when they are perfectly dry and just at their best.

TO PRESERVE: The whole stem should be lightly pressed between blotting paper.

GALTONIA CANDICANS

COMMON NAME **Summer hyacinth**
FAMILY *Liliaceae*

A native of Africa, this plant is a great favourite of mine – I always long to make a shower bouquet entirely from the creamy-white bell flowers. Unfortunately these cannot be preserved in any way, but air-drying the candelabra-shaped seedheads seems to work well.

TO PRESERVE: Pick the seedheads as soon as the last flower has faded, unless it is a warm summer, in which case they will ripen well on the plant. Hang upside down to dry.

GERANIUM

FAMILY *Geraniaceae*

It is the scented leaves that are of main interest in this plant. They are excellent in potpourris and many will preserve successfully. Some of the seedheads may be dried for use in arrangements but they are brittle and need careful handling.

TO PRESERVE: Deeply lobed or coloured leaves will press well between sheets of blotting paper. Air-dry seedheads.

GLADIOLUS

FAMILY *Iridaceae*

At the end of the season, remaining uncut stems may produce long-stemmed seedheads which dry well.

TO PRESERVE: Remove seedheads when lifting corms for storage and hang up to air-dry.

GODETIA

FAMILY *Onagraceae*

This hardy annual produces a useful flower spike in the form of a seedhead. Unfortunately, the flowers, which are very large and soft, do not dry well although once the seed pods develop the whole stem is worth keeping.

TO PRESERVE: Remove the leaves and hang the seedheads up to dry.

GOMPHRENA

FAMILY *Amaranthaceae*

This flower, much favoured in the nineteenth century, has recently found its way back into the commercial cut-flower trade. The papery-textured flowers come in a wide range of colours from deep blue to yellow, white and purple, and from a distance look similar to clover. Gomphrena is a half-hardy annual and will stand a little forcing under glass, which will give it extra stem length.

TO PRESERVE: Cut as soon as the flowers are fully open, then hang them upside down to air-dry.

GRASSES

FAMILY *Gramineae*

A huge family of some 5,000 species which, despite their ready availability, are all too often ignored as flower decorations. Yet there is nothing nicer than having a few seedheads of grass in a simple arrangement of dried garden flowers – they will lighten and add height to the whole decoration. Endless forms of seedheads can be used from giant pampas heads to the fine heads of annual meadow grass. All dry well. Harvest some early to retain the grey-green colouring and others later, for the golden hues.

TO PRESERVE: Hang up to air-dry in small bunches. Once dry lay flat and keep in boxes. Some will store much more easily than others – the fine filmy seedheads are the most difficult.

GYPSOPHILA

COMMON NAME **Baby's breath**
FAMILY *Caryophyllaceae*

This plant is suddenly enjoying new popularity, and appears in many arrangements and bouquets. The double form *Gypsophila paniculata* var. "Bristol Fairy" is the best one to dry – the annual single flower *Gypsophila elegans* is larger and tends to look untidy when tucked into a dry arrangement. It seems nowadays that there is no season for it because it is grown and exported from so many different parts of the world. Its normal flowering period in the garden is midsummer.

TO PRESERVE: Hang up bunches to air-dry.

HEBE (see VERONICA)

HEDERA

COMMON NAME **Ivy**
FAMILY *Araliaceae*

Perhaps one of the most useful foliage plants for both decorator and florist alike. It can be preserved by both pressing and the use of glycerine.

TO PRESERVE: Press the leaves and long sprays, though some may not keep their colour markings. Glycerine is an excellent means of preserving the trails of ivy which are so useful low down or at the sides of arrangements. Some of the naturally stiff pieces may even soften a little.

HELICHRYSUM

COMMON NAME **Straw flower**
FAMILY *Compositae*

Perhaps the most popular genus of all dried flowers, and one that is easily obtainable. Helichrysum comes in a number of forms – some are annual, some perennial – and one or two are grown more for their foliage than their flowers. The most popular is *Helichrysum bracteatum*. The flowers, which appear in early August, come in white and many other strong colours and are easy to grow. Treated as a half-hardy annual, helichrysum needs a good sunny period in which to grow well and then plenty of sun to ripen off the flowers at the end of the season.

TO PRESERVE: Cut off the early flowers with short stems to encourage the plant to go on growing. Remove the mature blooms before they are fully open and wire up the short stems, air-drying them in a warm, dark place. The second crop of flowers will be a little smaller and often more attractive than the first. Pick these before the flower centre becomes visible as they seem to continue to grow and open once they're wired up. At the end of the season, cut the long stems and bring in to dry. Remove all the leaves at the base of the stem but leave a few thin ones around the flowers.

You will often see bunches of helichrysum sold as fresh flowers in flower shops in the late summer. Tie them up as soon as you get home and hang up to air-dry straight away.

HELIPTERUM MANGLESII

FAMILY *Compositae*

A half-hardy annual native to Australia, often known as *Rhodanthe manglesii*. It is one of the earliest of the dried flowers to be harvested, usually being ready by early summer. The silver-pink buds are most attractive, more so, in fact, than the really open flowers, which range from pink to white in colour and have a yellow centre. The large number of blooms on each stem ensures a good range of flower sizes at each picking.

TO PRESERVE: Hang up to air-dry in warm moving air.

HERACLEUM

COMMON NAMES **Hogweed, Cow parsnip**
FAMILY *Umbelliferae*

A most impressive and decorative plant which should be dried whenever available, though it should be handled with care, as it can cause a skin rash. *Heracleum mantegazzianum* will grow up to 8 feet (2.4 metres) tall and a fully developed specimen is quite impossible to handle as one main stem. The wild carrot (*Daucus carota*, another *Umbelliferae*) is much smaller, and its green seedheads are excellent: the stems seem to curve over to form a green lacy ball. These seedheads often feature in window dressings and at Christmas time may well be whitened and then frosted with glitter. There is no doubt that they make very dramatic decorations for large areas.

TO PRESERVE: Air-dry after the seedheads have formed.

HERBS

A very loose term, referring to many families and species. A number of common garden herbs may be cut and air-dried to use in mixed decorations and also in potpourris. The seedheads of rue (*Ruta graveolens*) are most attractive, and herbs such as rosemary (*Rosmarinus*) and mint (*Mentha*) give off excellent aromatic properties when rubbed up before adding to potpourri.

TO PRESERVE: Cut at the end of the growing season and air-dry.

HOSTA

COMMON NAME **Plantain lily**
FAMILY *Liliaceae*

A great favourite with flower-arrangers.

TO PRESERVE: The smaller, well-formed and coloured leaves may be pressed and these will keep well. After flowering, allow the seedheads to develop and when swollen, cut them and dry by hanging up to air-dry.

HUMULUS

COMMON NAME **Hop**
FAMILY *Cannabiaceae*

A most decorative climbing plant, humulus is not grown in gardens much these days, though there are still some wild varieties to be found in certain parts of the country. It is not easy to handle and its abrasive stems can cause a skin rash.

TO PRESERVE: Pick as the flower heads turn gold, remove every leaf and air-dry.

HYDRANGEA

FAMILY *Hydrangeaceae*

An excellent and versatile plant for drying. Hydrangeas come in beautiful colours, especially towards the autumn when the colour intensity seems to show up well in the cooler temperatures. The various hues include white, green, deep blue, and an almost beetroot red. I particularly like the metallic shades which look wonderful with pewter.

TO PRESERVE: Pick as the petals of the flowers begin to feel a little papery. You may treat them in a number of ways, all of which are successful. Hang upside down to air-dry or place in a little water and allow to water-dry as an arrangement. Some people like to dry small heads in sand and you can also preserve them in glycerine. However be sure to remove all but a few leaves because these do not dry well. (When using glycerine or water-drying, a few leaves around the head help to draw up the fluid.) Once dry, the flower heads last for a very long time if not handled.

RECOMMENDED SPECIES: *H. macrophylla* and *H. paniculata*.

IBERIS

COMMON NAME **Candytuft**
FAMILY *Cruciferae*

This annual plant produces an excellent seedhead for drying. Grow some for cutting in full flower, when they will make most attractive fresh flower arrangements, but keep some spare plants for seed production.

TO PRESERVE: Cut seedheads as soon as the flowers are over and hang up to air-dry. Some people varnish lightly for a slightly different effect.

IRIS

FAMILY *Iridaceae*

A group of herbaceous perennials, of which some will grow well in shady conditions and others need full sun. Unfortunately, the flowers themselves do not dry or press, but their sword-like leaves and range of different-sized seed-heads can be preserved very successfully. The little pointed leaves of the *Iris sibirica* are very small and pretty, and *I. foetidissima* (the stinking iris) provides the most striking seedhead. This should be cut when the pods are just splitting and brought in to air-dry. At the same time paint over the berries with varnish or gum arabic to hold the bright orange seeds in place. The common Water Flag, *I. pseudacorus* produces enormous seed pods which hang beautifully in a large group. A number of irises have variegated foliage which, if preserved, will be an added bonus to any dried group.

TO PRESERVE: Press the leaves. See above for instructions on preserving the seedhead.

ISATIS TINCTORIA

COMMON NAME **Dyer's woad**
FAMILY *Cruciferae*

An old-fashioned plant formerly used for making a blue dye. This biennial is useful for large groups. When in flower it is attractive as fresh material, but do save some stems for the unusual seedheads which are excellent for drying. They are somewhat untidy in appearance, but will add interest to a really big group.

TO PRESERVE: The long stiff stems dry perfectly by hanging upside down to air-dry.

JUNCUS

COMMON NAME **Bog rush**
FAMILY *Juncaceae*

Reeds and rushes will provide excellent dried materials in the form of seedheads. They are, however, difficult to handle and the stems, which are often hollow, break easily.

TO PRESERVE: Hang up to air-dry with plenty of room. This is a slow process but is worth doing. It may pay to run a wire up some of the stems to hold them straight.

LAURUS NOBILIS

COMMON NAME **Sweet bay**
FAMILY *Lauraceae*

A decorative tree from the Mediterranean area, this is an excellent aromatic evergreen which will dry, press or take up glycerine. It is a most useful tree to have in the garden but do allow it plenty of room – many people have it trimmed in Versailles tubs and do not realize the ultimate size it will reach in only a short time. To use in its green form or as backing foliage, cut the well-formed shoots. For potpourri all you need is dried individual leaves which are shredded. Any leaves not perfect for use in floristry may be used in the kitchen.

TO PRESERVE: Air-dry or press the leaves, or use glycerine on stems.

LAVANDULA

COMMON NAME **Lavender**
FAMILY *Labiatae*

An old-fashioned favourite, featuring in the street cries of old London. There are a number of plants in the group, both shrubby and herbaceous: *Lavandula spica* is one of the most successful. Lavender is best known for its scent. It does also make a pleasing hedge of slow growth but will require a good soil in a sunny position. It is excellent in small dried arrangements and posies and the scented heads may be used in potpourri.

TO PRESERVE: Pick or cut before the blue flowers are fully open and lay out or hang up to air-dry. (If you pick before the flower opens it has a strange scent.)

LEONTOPODIUM ALPINUM

COMMON NAME **Edelweiss**
FAMILY *Compositae*

Another great favourite – well worth growing and drying. It will grow well in open ground but it must have well-drained soil and a good sunny aspect.

TO PRESERVE: Cut just before the centre opens to a fluffy mass. Air-dry or dry in fine sand.

LIATRIS

COMMON NAME **Blazing star**
FAMILY *Compositae*

The stiff purple flower spike of this plant seems so hard compared with other fresh flowers, but, in its dried form, it softens and provides useful colour. It is now available all over the world and thus never has a true season. I have seen it for sale in Holland, New Zealand and on the side of the Grand Canal in Venice on a small outdoor flower stand.

TO PRESERVE: Hang up the flower spike to air-dry.

LILIUM

COMMON NAME **Lily**
FAMILY *Liliaceae*

This is a very large family with many different forms to choose from. The seed-heads are most useful, and can really add a great deal of interest in a large group. The stems of *Lilium giganteum* (*Cardiocrinum giganteum*) can grow to 8–9 feet (2.4–2.7 metres) but you are unlikely to come by many of these. Do, however, try to get hold of a number of different seedheads for interesting shapes. The pods seem to colour well with *L. pyrenaicum* in particular being very varied. Strip off the foliage before drying or, if you have plenty of room, allow the whole stems to dry, then rub off the leaves at a later stage.

TO PRESERVE: Cut the seedheads off the plant before they are ready to split and stand them up in containers to air-dry.

LIMONIUM

COMMON NAMES **Sea lavender, Statice, Dumosa**
FAMILY *Plumbaginaceae*

A perennial plant which does well in dry weather: all forms are excellent for drying. Its small, many-coloured flowers will grow best in open sandy conditions. The flower stem is much branched and similar in habit to gypsophila. *Limonium sinuatum* is the best known of all dried flowers: it is a perennial grown as an annual, providing many stems of much branched habit in a good season. *L. suworowii* is also a very well-known dried flower: it can be grown from seed and will do well if it can enjoy a quick growing period in full sun.

TO PRESERVE: Cut all species when the flowers are just showing and hang up to air-dry.

LUNARIA

COMMON NAMES **Honesty, Money plant**
FAMILY *Cruciferae*

An old-established and popular dried material. Lunaria is usually treated as a biennial. It will grow from seed and will thrive quite well in partial shade. It is for its seed pods that it is grown and sold on the commercial market. Unfortunately it often appears today with the silvery moon-shaped membranes dividing the seed pods dyed in the most awful colours. Trim out the compound heads and save the small pieces for small arrangements. The long stems will be good in large groups. Once established, a few seeds will usually drop each year to carry on the crop.

TO PRESERVE: Pick when the pods are fully developed but before the seeds turn really dark and stain the central membrane. Hang up to air-dry. When ready the seed pod coats will lift and fall from the central membrane.

MAHONIA

COMMON NAME **Berberis**
FAMILY *Berberidaceae*

A group of evergreen shrubs which have excellent pinnate or compound leaves.

They are glossy and ornate, ideal when dried for the centre of a mixed green group or in Christmas decorations. The flowers are scented but not long-lasting and appear at the end of winter.

TO PRESERVE: Pick the individual compound leaves and press – they are leathery and will take some time to dry.

MATRICARIA

FAMILY *Compositae*

The plants in this family are mostly wild. The most worthwhile species for drying purposes is *Matricaria eximia*, probably best known by its synonym *Chrysanthemum parthenium*.

TO PRESERVE: These small flower heads will dry well in sand and also by hanging upside down and air-drying. They tend to curl a little but can still make a useful addition to a small group.

MOLUCELLA LAEVIS

COMMON NAMES **Bells of Ireland, Shell-flower**
FAMILY *Labiatae*

This plant, perhaps one of the best known of the dried flowers, is an annual which can easily be grown in a reasonably good summer. It will need plenty of sun and a fairly dry soil. Imported stems (from Kenya, Israel and South America) are available in quite large quantities and at any time of the year. Beautiful as these plants are however, they have very tall stems and can really only be used in large groups.

TO PRESERVE: The stems respond to glycerine treatment and also to air-drying by hanging. The young bells tend to shrivel so pick them when the maximum number of flowers are out. If too old you will find that the bells at the base of the typically square stem will drop off in the drying process. I would recommend just a little glycerine treatment followed by air-drying – this seems to make the stems less brittle. Some people advocate drying in silica or sand, but I find that this is suitable only for the very small stems – the larger ones are simply too awkward to handle in this way. If the bells drop off, they can be glued back into position.

MONARDA DIDYMA

COMMON NAMES **Sweet bergamot, Bee balm**
FAMILY *Labiatae*

A member of the nettle family that has a fragrance which is useful in potpourri. Although it loses its shape somewhat during drying, the flower works well in a mixed group. This summer-flowering plant is often seen in herbaceous borders.

TO PRESERVE: Pick when the petals are fully out and air-dry by hanging or laying on a wire frame.

MUSCARI

COMMON NAME **Grape hyacinth**
FAMILY *Liliaceae*

This wild flower of the Mediterranean region is excellent for dried arrangements. Many people will have seen the seed pods — perhaps without knowing what they are — during summer holidays on the Greek Islands. These papery pods may be on stems up to 12 inches (30 centimetres) high. They are fragile and should be handled with the greatest of care. Muscari are one of the most useful of the bulb flowers but may be overlooked in the garden because by the time they are ready, so much more plant growth will have appeared which may well have smothered them.

TO PRESERVE: Leave to dry naturally on the plant or pick when nearly dry and hang up to dry off completely in the air.

NARCISSUS

COMMON NAME **Daffodil**
FAMILY *Amaryllidaceae*

I always think of these as essentially fresh flowers although many will dry well. In general, the deeper the colour in their natural form, the better this will hold when dried.

TO PRESERVE: It is not easy to dictate how to do the drying other than to say that while the miniature bulb flowers may be treated whole, the larger flowered varieties should be cut from their stems before treating. Both should be laid in silica gel or dried sand. The time taken to

dry varies and they will need constant monitoring. If the flowers are removed too soon they will collapse and rot; if left too long, they become very brittle. Many people wire the heads first because this makes handling easier.

NEPETA

COMMON NAME **Catmint**
FAMILY *Labiatae*

This well-known herbaceous plant is worth cutting when in flower and drying. It has a fragrance which will add to the group. The lilac-blue flowers should be just beginning to open when cutting takes place.

TO PRESERVE: Hang up to air-dry.

NICANDRA PHYSALODES

COMMON NAMES **Apple of Peru, Shoo-fly plant**
FAMILY *Solanaceae*

This annual plant is really a weed, but it is so attractive that I feel it's worth growing in the border. The bell-shaped blue flower is somewhat insignificant but the overall effect of the plant when the pods have formed is very decorative. It is similar to *Datura* in its habit of growth but the seed pods are very similar to those of the Chinese lantern (*Physalis*).

TO PRESERVE: Air-dry by hanging up in freely-circulating air.

NIGELLA

COMMON NAMES **Love-in-a-mist, Fennel flower**
FAMILY *Ranunculaceae*

This annual from the Mediterranean area is useful in its dried flower form, when its blue, white and pink hues add colour to a summer group. The seed pod stage is even more attractive. Some people recommend that these be varnished, but I prefer the natural matt finish.

TO PRESERVE: Remove most of the leaves and hang the stems up to air-dry. The flowers will dry well in sand — cut the stems and lay them in boxes. The seed

pods are often dried as an entire plant, in their natural clusters — they may be cut up as required later on.

ORIGANUM

COMMON NAME **Sweet marjoram**
FAMILY *Labiatae*

Another member of the nettle family, this aromatic herb dries excellently when in flower, keeping its colour well. The purplish rounded flowers and bracts make interesting shapes in a mixed group.

TO PRESERVE: Air-dry.

PAEONIA

COMMON NAME **Peony**
FAMILY *Paeoniaceae, formerly Ranunculaceae*

These are truly beautiful in their many forms. Some of the flowers can be dried in desiccants but this is not easy to do: the small single flowers of the tree peony are perhaps the easiest to tackle. The foliage of the tree peonies, too, is very useful for its shape and colour, and this will press well. Some of the herbaceous peony foliage colours beautifully in the early autumn, and this too may well press successfully. The lovely seed pods can also be dried.

TO PRESERVE: Dry flower heads in desiccants and press foliage as described above. Air-dry seed pods.

PAPAVER

COMMON NAME **Poppy**
FAMILY *Papaveraceae*

Poppies are striking but unfortunately the blooms cannot be preserved. The coloured and shaped seed pods, however, are excellent in dried arrangements.

TO PRESERVE: Allow the pods to dry in the garden and, when ready, cut them, strip off the faded foliage and hang upside down to air-dry. At this stage the seed will shed. Continue to hang to dry fully.

PHLOMIS FRUTICOSA

COMMON NAME **Jerusalem sage**
FAMILY *Labiatae*

An unusual plant normally grown in a herbaceous border or at the front of a shrubbery. Its soft greenish-grey foliage and pale yellow flowers arranged in whorls up the square stems make it an interesting subject. Its seedheads are useful in a mixed collection.

TO PRESERVE: Take off the rather untidy leaves from the base of each whorl of seed capsules and hang up to air-dry.

PHYSALIS

COMMON NAMES **Chinese lantern, Cape gooseberry**
FAMILY *Solanaceae*

Again, well-known for its use as dried material. Physalis tends to spread rapidly when grown in the border, so it must be controlled in a special bed. The swollen orange/yellow calyx is rather like a lantern in shape and when well-grown can be quite attractive. It is, however, important to harvest at the correct time – so often the slugs play havoc with the papery lanterns and one is then left with a net-like calyx which is not attractive. These are really best in large groups – the normal-sized lanterns are too large for small arrangements.

TO PRESERVE: Cut when colour is turning and hang up to air-dry but do remember to hang them with stems down, so that the lanterns hang correctly when dry. They dry quite quickly. Remove the leaves and soft tips to the stem. The lanterns will glue back on easily if they become detached.

PLANTAGO

COMMON NAME **Plantain**
FAMILY *Plantaginaceae*

The members of this family are mostly troublesome weeds. Those found in lawns are of little use in dried arrangements but *Plantago major*, found in the countryside, has a long slender green-brown seedhead which curves and takes on interesting lines.

TO PRESERVE: Air-dry the seedheads. Some people like to varnish them to give them extra quality.

POTENTILLA ANSERINA

FAMILY *Rosaceae*

A particularly pretty wild flower with a most attractive silver foliage. The shape of the leaf varies somewhat. It tends to be star-shaped in outline, but the points can be of different lengths. The leaves are useful in mixed arrangements.

TO PRESERVE: Press the leaves as soon as they are picked. They may also be treated with glycerine.

PRIMULA

FAMILY *Primulaceae*

Many primulas – and there are hundreds of them – produce interesting seedheads at the end of the flowering season. The ones we have used in this book are polyanthuses: garden hybrids derived from *Primula vulgaris* and *P. veris*.

TO PRESERVE: Collect when the stems have really dried on the plant but before they become too discoloured. Continue air-drying by standing the stems upright in a small empty container.

PROTEA

FAMILY *Proteaceae*

A flower native to tropical and southern Africa. Magnificent protea are available in all sizes and many colours: perhaps the most attractive is *Protea serruria*, var. "Blushing Bride". Small and just off-white with a touch of pink to the outside row of petals, it is quite the most dainty of all the protea and worth looking for.

TO PRESERVE: Air-dry as an arrangement.

PRUNUS

COMMON NAME **Plum cherry**
FAMILY *Rosaceae*

A very large group of trees and shrubs supplying much useful dried foliage material for the decorator. The two main foliages are *Prunus laurocerasus* (laurel) and *P. lusitanica* (Portugal laurel). Both can be pressed or treated with glycerine when they will take up a very rich dark colour; individual leaves may also be preserved for bouquets and floristry work. The fruits will not hold well, however. The deep red *P. cerasifera*, var. "Atropurpurea" is excellent pressed or treated with glycerine but must be collected early in the season before it becomes shredded from insect damage. The individual flowers of some of the ornamental cherries are worth preserving in silica gel – they should be wired before going into the drying agent. I cannot see why the long flower spikes of *P. padus* (bird cherry) would not respond well to treatment in glycerine just as the first flowers are coming out, though I have not tried this myself. Remove a number of the leaves on each stem, as their thick and heavy appearance will obscure the dainty effect of the flowers.

TO PRESERVE: Treat leaves, stems and flowers as described above.

RHEUM RHAPONTICUM

COMMON NAME **Rhubarb**
FAMILY *Polygonaceae*

Do not attempt to dry the leaves! Drying the flower heads in full seed, though, is worthwhile.

TO PRESERVE: Spray lightly with lacquer or varnish just to hold the heavy seedheads together. Hang upside down to air-dry.

RHODODENDRON

FAMILY *Ericaceae*

Constance Spry was wonderful at using anything that was unusual, and whenever she used the spent flower heads of the large rhododendron in an arrangement it always caused interest – even though many people did not know what they were. I have even seen them used in a bouquet. Collect seedheads of rhododendron at the end of the season and dry them – they will add interest and beauty to your arrangement.

TO PRESERVE: Air-dry. They are of course best taken off the shrub on natural stems. If you cannot afford to cut too much off your bush, you may wire up some on false stems.

RHUS

COMMON NAME **Sumach**
FAMILY *Anacardiaceae*

There are a number of different rhus but the two most commonly found are *Rhus typhina* and *R. cotinus*. *R. typhina* has the most beautiful autumn colours. Its compound pinnate leaves are well worth pressing. Air-dry the flower spikes at the end of the season when they have turned into a deep red seed cluster. The smoke tree *R. cotinus* (syn. *Cotinus coggygria*), is also wonderful for its autumn colouring and smoky grey panicles, but these are difficult to retain. The small round individual leaves will press well but do not bear any likeness to those on the tree in the autumn.

TO PRESERVE: Press and air-dry as above.

ROSA

COMMON NAME **Rose**
FAMILY *Rosaceae*

There are so many members of this family that one would like to preserve, but many of them do not dry well. Some do, however, and bunches of dried roses are on sale in many stores which stock dry flowers. They tend to be brittle and much darker than when fresh. Both roses from the garden or bunches of commercial varieties can be air-dried. It is best to do this quickly, using roses barely past the bud stage, in a warm place. An airing cupboard is ideal, if you have room.

TO PRESERVE: For long-stemmed varieties, hang up the stems with the heads pointing downwards, having removed a few of the base leaves first. For short-stemmed roses, try threading the stems through a rack of 2 inch (5 centimetre) wire netting. Just rest the heads on the netting frame covered with a layer of tissue paper to save bruising the bottom petals. An alter-

native method is to dry in sand, but the rose must be perfectly dry before it is placed in the sand. This method takes four to seven days. Some people use silica gel. This must be carefully dusted in around the base of the petals, which should be dry and in perfect condition. Leave the short-stemmed-flowers resting in an upward-facing position, having first wired them to make false stems. They will take three to eight days to dry out.

RUDBECKIA

COMMON NAME **Coneflower**
FAMILY *Compositae*

These small sunflower-like blooms are quite easy to preserve for large winter decorations.

TO PRESERVE: Perfect specimens should be picked and allowed to dry out around the flower head, while the stems must be kept in water to prevent wilting. Place in sand or silica gel, face downwards, having first carefully laid the petals out in one complete flat ring. Wire the small piece of stem before starting to dry. Do remember to keep drying out the sand – if it's doing its job properly it will soon become damp itself.

RUMEX

COMMON NAMES **Dock, sorrel**
FAMILY *Polygonaceae*

Most of the plants that we know well in this group are weeds. Some are a real nuisance, yet to the dried flower collector they offer many interesting seedheads and foliages. (Unfortunately this is an easy way of spreading them around from garden to garden – what started as an attractive gift may turn out to be a pest! Perhaps the best thing to do is to burn the old seedheads after use rather than placing them on a compost heap – it is amazing how long certain seedheads can remain intact and dormant.) The great water dock (*Rumex hydrolapathum*) produces fine seedheads which are excellent in large groups and many others adopt a wonderful colouring in the autumn. The plants of this group are usually found growing in acid soils, and are worth collecting and handling with care. Some require very little drying because they naturally dry well on the plant.

TO PRESERVE: Remove the foliage then hang the seedheads upside down to air-dry.

RUTA GRAVEOLENS

COMMON NAME **Rue**
FAMILY *Rutaceae*

This excellent perennial herb is well worth pressing. The attractive grey-green-silver foliage has aromatic properties and individual leaves in particular will work well in small arrangements. The small flower inflorescence is rather insignificant but it may be cut out of the growing point at the end of the season and air-dried. "Jackman's Blue" is the best variety to grow, although it does not always keep its colour when pressed.

TO PRESERVE: Press or air-dry.

SALIX CAPREA

COMMON NAME **Pussy willow**
FAMILY *Salicaceae*

These can now be bought in artificial form but unfortunately the stems come in mixed colours. Try cutting and drying natural pussy willow when it is well formed – you will find that even though it does shrivel slightly its shape and beauty can still be appreciated. Salix is excellent for giving a "line" to medium or large arrangements.

TO PRESERVE: Hang up to air-dry or treat lightly with glycerine.

SALVIA

COMMON NAME **Sage**
FAMILY *Labiatae*

This group includes a great range of plants ranging from annuals to shrubby materials. Many have flower spikes in a range of colours; these come at the end of the flower season and must be well formed before they are picked. Add the aromatic leaves to potpourri.

TO PRESERVE: Air-dry the flower spikes.

SANTOLINA

COMMON NAME **Cotton lavender**
FAMILY *Compositae*

Small grey-white leaves with flat yellow button flower heads make this a useful species for drying.

TO PRESERVE: Cut the short stems, bunch and hang up to air-dry.

SCABIOSA

COMMON NAME **Paper moon**
FAMILY *Dipsacaceae*

This is a pretty plant with soft lavender leaves, which are shed to leave a round seedhead made up of papery spheres. These seedheads are most attractive in mixed arrangements.

TO PRESERVE: Hang up to air-dry.

SEDUM

COMMON NAME **Ice plant**
FAMILY *Crassulaceae*

The flat heads of the ice plant make interesting seedheads at the end of the flowering season.

TO PRESERVE: Pick well before the stems go soft, then remove the fleshy leaves and hang up to air-dry.

SILENE VULGARIS

COMMON NAME **Bladder campion**
FAMILY *Caryophyllaceae*

It is the balloon-shaped side capsules of this plant that are of interest.

TO PRESERVE: Cut when the capsules are well-formed and hang up to air-dry. At this stage they will still be in their green form. Later, when the flower has set seed, the capsule will turn brown. It may be worthwhile carefully painting them with varnish when still green, then laying them carefully until the varnish dries.

SOLIDAGO

COMMON NAME **Goldenrod**
FAMILY *Compositae*

This plant is a weed in some parts of the world, but the dried flower stems or side shoots can be useful. There are a number of different yellows to be obtained and the flower spikes also vary slightly.

TO PRESERVE: Cut when just turning into flower and air-dry by hanging up, having first removed all the leaves. The flowers tend to open while being dried.

SPIRAEA

FAMILY *Rosaceae*

The flat seedheads of *Spiraea bullata bumalda*, var. "Anthony Waterer", and of *Spiraea douglasii* are good for drying and should be cut once the flower is over. It is also worth trying a few stems of each of these species just as they come into flower – by doing so you may be able to retain their colour. Wild Spiraea and those from the herbaceous border will also produce good seedheads.

TO PRESERVE: Hang up to air-dry, having first rubbed off leaves on the woody stem. Dry fairly quickly.

STACHYS LANATA

COMMON NAME **Lamb's tongue**
FAMILY *Labiatae*

These soft, felt-like grey foliage plants make useful material. Do not attempt to dry the flower stem, just the young shoots.

TO PRESERVE: Air-dry the young foliage shoots in a horizontal position, turning regularly, or treat with glycerine.

STATICE (see LIMONIUM)

SYRINGA

COMMON NAME **Lilac**
FAMILY *Oleaceae*

This plant's attractive flowers cannot be preserved. The seedheads however, will dry successfully. *Syringa vulgaris* provides the best.

TO PRESERVE: Cut the seedheads at the end of the season and hang up to air-dry.

TAGETES

COMMON NAME **Marigold**
FAMILY *Compositae*

Both *Tagetes erecta* (African marigold) and *T. patula* (French marigold) make useful dried materials.

TO PRESERVE: Wire the flower heads and set them, facing downwards, in silica gel or sand. Large flower varieties will also air-dry successfully.

TANACETUM VULGARE

COMMON NAME **Tansy**
FAMILY *Compositae*

This wild flower – a perennial herb much used in former times for its medicinal properties – is only occasionally seen today in herb gardens. The strong-smelling flower head is made up of many deep yellow button-like structures with no petals. The foliage is similar to that of *Achillea* and other members of the *Compositae* family. It is useful in both large and small arrangements.

TO PRESERVE: Cut just as the flowers come into full colour. Remove all foliage from the stems, then hang up to air-dry.

THISTLE

FAMILY *Compositae*

A term applied to a number of wild and cultivated herbaceous plants of the *Compositae* family with spiny leaves and spiny, tufted flower heads. Although difficult to handle, they are well worth collecting. Some are pretty, even after the flower has opened and shattered.

TO PRESERVE: Wearing gloves, and using a sharp knife or secateurs, cut before the flower head is fully open as the process of developing and opening will go on as it dries. Remove any thorns and leaves, then hang up to dry. The papery silver calyx is very useful in a wide number of decorations.

RECOMMENDED SPECIES: *Onopordom acanthium* (Scotch thistle), *Silybum marianum* (milk-thistle) and *Carlina vulgaris* (Carline thistle).

TULIPA

COMMON NAME **Tulip**
FAMILY *Liliaceae*

This is only worth drying if you really feel like a challenge! The time and money involved may not make it worthwhile – and in any case very good silk reproductions of tulips are now available. The seed pods, on the other hand, will dry easily and successfully.

TO PRESERVE: Gather the seed pods at the end of the flowering season and stand upright in a dry container to air-dry. For those wishing to attempt drying the flower, pick the bud just as the petals are opening. Half-fill a container with drying agent (sand or silica) and lay the flower on this, stem end down, then cover over with more drying agent until the base of the flower is held firmly in shape.

TYPHA ANGUSTIFOLIA

COMMON NAME **Lesser reedmace**
FAMILY *Typhaceae*

These slender rushes are far more attractive than the really thick bulrush or great reedmace (*Typha latifolia*) – everything is daintier and easier to handle. Treat with great care to prevent any damage to the

brown fruiting head with its velvety coat. Should this split, enormous quantities of fluff and seed will be released.

TO PRESERVE: Cut when the brown fruit heads are fully developed and the male flowers at the top of the thick velvety rush are in bloom. Spray carefully with hair lacquer and dry off in an airy dry place.

VERBASCUM

COMMON NAME **Mullein**
FAMILY *Scrophulariaceae*

This wild and cultivated plant has extremely attractive soft grey/silver leaves. It is often found growing in chalky areas and is really a biennial, with a primrose yellow flower spike appearing in the second year.

TO PRESERVE: Air-dry: the open flowers will drop but the buds will remain with some yellow colouring.

VERONICA

COMMON NAME **Speedwell**
FAMILY *Scrophulariaceae*

TO PRESERVE: The herbaceous forms produce good flower spikes which may be air-dried or placed to dry in sand. The shrubby species (genus *Hebe*) may also be dried – try drying these in silica or sand.

VIBURNUM

FAMILY *Caprifoliaceae*

Many small trees and shrubs in this species give enjoyment in the flower-arranging world – the early winter *Viburnum fragrans* (syn. *V. farreri*) and then, in the early spring, the guelder rose *V. opulus* (var. "Sterile") from Holland, with its sharp green pompom flower heads, are just two that come to mind.

TO PRESERVE: All species may be dried in silica gel, though great care is required in this. Some of the attractive autumnal colouring on the leaves may be retained by carefully pressing.

XERANTHEMUM

COMMON NAME **Immortelle**
FAMILY *Compositae*

A group of annuals native to the Mediterranean. When picked and dried the flowers last for many years (hence their common name) and will retain their colour well. The star-shaped flowers range from white and pink to purple. They are borne by the plant between August and the early frosts in winter.

TO PRESERVE: Hang up to air-dry. In a warm, dry summer, the flowers will dry naturally on the plant.

ZINNIA

FAMILY *Compositae*

The Zinnia is an excellent flower which thrives in plenty of sunlight. Most are native to Mexico. Zinnia does best in hot dry conditions, when it will grow very rapidly.

TO PRESERVE: These plants have magnificent colourings which are retained well when dried in sand or silica gel. Cut when fully open but before the pollen is being shed. Remove heads and wire before drying carefully in the chosen desiccant.